Fermenter

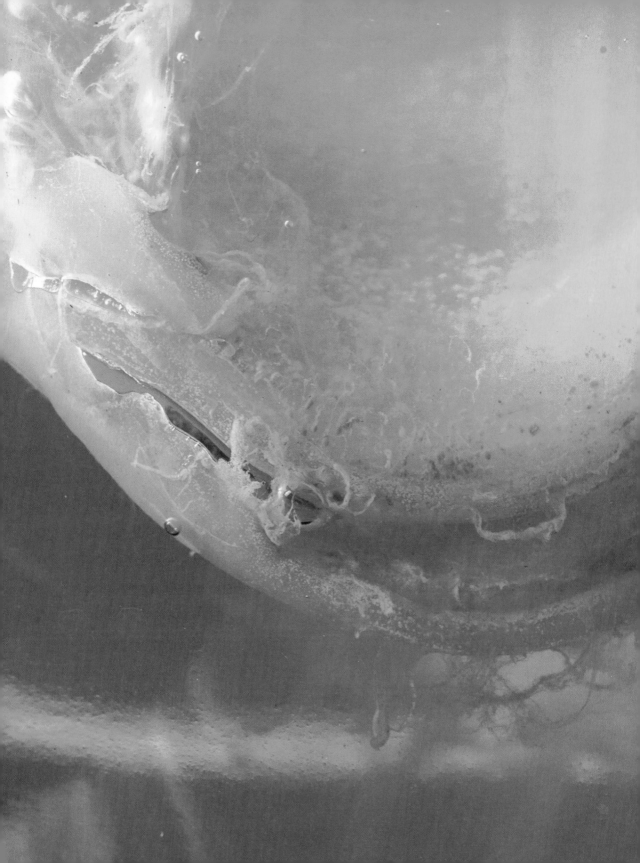

FERMENTER

DIY FERMENTATION FOR VEGAN FARE

Aaron Adams

Liz Crain

photos by
George Barberis

SASQUATCH BOOKS
SEATTLE

CONTENTS

RECIPES

PART 1

FERMENTS

PART 2

DISHES

Foreword

When I first heard that Aaron was writing the *Fermenter* cookbook, I was ecstatic. Fermenter is hands down one of my favorite restaurants in the country, and luckily, I live just a few blocks away. It's a groundbreaking establishment that rejects any notion of the old-school vegan cafés I still find myself in around the country in favor of cuisine with wildly delicious, local, organic, and seasonal ferments at the core. To visit the restaurant and workshop is to take a trip around the world of fermentation. In the corner, pink orbs of koji fuzz–covered beets take us to Japan. The adjacent trays are lined with perfect blocks of bean-and-seed-studded tempeh, and you can almost smell the Indonesian curry they call for. Mouths already watering, we get to the selections of fizzy and fruity kefirs and kombuchas. It's all very science lab, but warm and delicious. To take a tour of all the projects with Aaron, and the rapid-fire excitement he exudes, is like a kid showing you all their toys. "Here! Try this brie we made!" "Hold on, let's get you a flight of all the booch to try! Wait, you gotta taste this vinegar!"

Fermenter is not the vegan café you ate at in college. When Aaron and team take these oh-so-carefully-made items and turn them into delicious salads, sandwiches, and drinks, the results take your palate to another place—tart, tangy, acidic, complex, and full of umami. Fruits and vegetables are never this good on their own. The funny thing is there is nothing new about fermentation. Things have been fermenting before human life on earth and will continue to after we are long gone.

I originally met Aaron at his first Portland restaurant, Portobello Vegan Trattoria. I had moved to Portland a few years prior and gone through a major life change that included getting sober and cleaning up my diet. I gave up dairy, gluten, and red meat and started frequenting all the vegan spots in town because I knew I could eat much of the menu at these places. Portobello was a damn good restaurant in a town with no shortage of vegan options. I remember Aaron working the room, as we chefs do, and getting to know him. I was so taken by his flavors that I invited him to do a collaboration with us for the annual early fall vegan dinner we hosted where I was working. Over the years I continued to be a fan of his food, especially of how he and the team have continued to create and redefine over the past few years. My health journey hasn't stopped, and getting my fill of gut-healthy, probiotic-rich fermented foods is one way I still make up for the many years I battered my body.

I asked Aaron if this was a fermentation cookbook or a restaurant book and we agree it's both. But really, it's a blueprint to get started fermenting at home whether you will be making pickles for the first time or are a kimchi wizard.

You may be surprised to see how few ingredients are needed to get started with preparations like North Coast Kraut (page 45) and Hot Behind Hot Sauce (page 41). Fermentation is, after all, just time, patience, and a little science. You will be thankful for the detailed step-by-step instructions for bigger projects like Pinto Bean Tempeh (page 85) and Koji Beets (page 73). I know I am. I have explored various fermentation methods and have had ferments on my menus, but I learned new things in every single recipe of this vital book.

Aaron also walks us through it all—how to set yourself up for success and how to proceed when the unexpected happens—with his deft breakdown of the science behind fermentation and by providing key tools to help along the way.

What Aaron really does in this book is empower us. He shows us that even with the most precise method, things can and will go wrong, but it's OK. Even the occasional failure teaches us and informs the next project. That's how all cooking works. And so does life. But when everything clicks, something incredible happens. And with a fridge and pantry stocked with a sundry of fermented foods, your cooking game transforms. Your family, friends, and health will thank you for it.

-Gregory Gourdet, James Beard Award–winning author of *Everyone's Table*, chef and founder of Kann Restaurant, and *Top Chef* All-Star

Oh, Hello There.

Most days when I'm behind the counter, I'll get some eager person, wild-eyed and firing fermentation questions at me. They want me to explain the mechanism for all the weird shit that's going on in all these jars and crocks, and most of the time I shrug and say, "I dunno." This, of course, usually doesn't go over that well, so I'll wryly add, "I approach fermentation from a craft perspective."

Indeed. Which is to say I'm a bit of a dum-dum who doesn't really know what the heck I'm doing. I can't imagine many old-timey fermenters understood exactly what was going on when they were salting cabbage and storing it away in big mud pots either, bless them. Knowing that gives me the strength I need to carry on making things when I have zero idea what's happening.

That's been a major theme in my life. As a moderately successful chef and restaurateur, who is pretty famous within the square block of Southeast Portland that Fermenter inhabits, I've always pushed forward into the inky darkness of not knowing. It isn't fearlessness or courage, but rather a sort of advantageous dim-wittedness that allows me to try all sorts of things out. Luckily, I also lack an ability to be too terribly embarrassed, which allows me to fail over and over again without slowing down.

This is an important trait for a fermenter. When some time ago I was having major texture deterioration issues with some cabbage kraut, I asked the experts

at The Cultured Pickle Shop in Berkeley, California (page 215), what I was doing
wrong. Kevin Farley, co-owner there with his wife, Alex Hozven, let me in on a little
secret when he said, "I imagine you will find, as we have, that fermentation is a cruel
collaborator, and will continue to fuck you over. Hopefully it will keep you humble."

And there you have it. Even the experts make something awful from time to time.
What I'm driving at here is, when you approach fermentation projects, be ready to
make some really disgusting things. Take plenty of notes so you can figure out what
the heck happened, and then try not to repeat those processes and re-create those
conditions. But don't ever, ever feel bad about trying.

I used to work for a chef who was a real asshole, but who did leave me with one
gem. He told me, "I'm not better than you, I've just fucked up more than you have." So,
go fuck stuff up, and make a million things. See which ones are good, and then hold on
to those babies.

WHO THE HECK ARE YOU?

I was raised in a fairly boring midsize town in the Bay Area named Livermore. After my parents divorced, we moved around a lot, landing in the great and noble city of Hayward in the East Bay. I spent a good amount of time there pissing off my parents, running around and hanging with other kids who liked pissing off their parents too. I was a fat, nerdy, somewhat androgynous, vegetarian weirdo, and I was unliked by most of my classmates. During my sophomore year of high school, I finally found a group of other weirdos who were having a hard time fitting in as well: punks.

Oh punks, beautiful punks. Even they had their hierarchies of cool, but a goofball like me could still find a way to wedge into their culture. I spent nearly every weekend at punk temple 924 Gilman in the early '90s. When I got beat up by a bunch of Nazis by the truck trailers down the street from Gilman, I joined a group of anti-racist kids called SHARP (Skinheads Against Racial Prejudice). After that, I went running around pretending to be a tough guy. Of course, I'm not very tough, and I remained fairly terrified while hanging out with these insane people for the next five years or so.

I continued my anti-racist skinhead gig when I moved up to Seattle, where I was very into wearing Levi's Sta-Prest trousers and red socks for many years. I am, as the kids say, over it now. (I know, I know: if you're not now, you never were. Oh well.)

I think that the first time I knew I wanted to cook (that is, to be a cook more than wanting to actually cook) was when I saw some swarthy-looking fellas in chef whites smoking cigarettes by a dumpster behind a restaurant. It had that same cachet as punk to me. Street tough and working class. I was instantly obsessed with kitchen culture, which I treated like any other subculture I obsessed over. I got my first kitchen job as a dishwasher at a terrible steakhouse where the chef wore cowboy boots and tried to impress the young waitresses by slinging kegs over his shoulder.

I went on to cook at many mediocre to fair restaurants throughout Seattle before wandering over to cook in a resort in Guam. I went from there to Miami, then New York City, then Jacksonville, Florida, and finally here to Portland, Oregon. Lots of stuff happened in all those places, but I've got to start talking about Fermenter here sooner than later, no?

Fermenter isn't a huge restaurant—we have just under 60 seats total inside and out, but we have really big hearts, and fermentation feeds so much of what we do. Fermenter's ethos centers around accessible, seasonal, handmade craft food made with local, organic agriculture and goods. We serve food that's craveable but also really good for you. Isn't that nice?

Fermenter also aims to make people feel good when they come in. Hospitality is an important aspect of being human with other humans. Making food without someone to make it for is pretty dreary.

I hope you agree when I say that everyone deserves dignity and respect. Cooking can do that for people. It is super-duper intimate, and you need to go about it responsibly. You are literally putting things into another person's body. And, if you're going to do that, you need to do it with consent. That is to say, if you say it's vegan and organic, you better damn well make sure it's vegan and organic. There are also some implied things in that consensual agreement, like, you know, not serving things that fell on the ground or that have broken glass in them.

If you think someone would be mad if they knew what you were feeding them, don't do it. But do make people feel welcome and offer them tasty and healthy things to eat. Maybe cooked up from this rad new book that you've got.

And, for the record, I 100 percent fully believe in keeping the Y in DIY. Do it yourself. Please. Make things! I won't hold your hand; you've gotta do the work, but I will give you a lot of advice, whether you ask for it or not.

I'll teach you how to be the blue-ribbon vegan at barbecues by bringing a big old bowl of our pickle-and-dill–loaded Fermenter Potato Salad (page 200), a stack of our BBQ Tempeh Sammies (page 169), a wheel of our hazelnutty Wine-Washed Aged Cheese (page 141), *and* a few chilled bottles of Fermenter's fizzy Raspberry–Lime Leaf Kefir (page 121) in your funny little tote bag. You know the one I'm talking about.

Then I'll go on and on about how to make the best gosh-dern vegan Reuben (Koji Beets, yo!) on the planet (page 159), and how to make all sorts of super-tasty kitchen staples like our Hot Behind Hot Sauce (page 41), North Coast Kraut (page 45), Chickpea Miso (page 61), Kombucha Honey (page 180), and Apple Cider Vinegar (page 100). In other words, I've got you.

OK, let's make some tasty food!

Getting Started

Before you get going on any of the book's ferments, Liz and I thought a short and sweet lowdown on the basics of fermentation, including a bit on how we do things at Fermenter, would be helpful.

One of the most important things to keep in mind with all ferments, not just ours, is that patience is key. Food and drink fermentation—even when it's a superfast ferment like our few-days Water Kefir (page 118), less-than-a-week Shio Koji (page 70), or our about-a-week krauts (pages 45–51)—is never going to be an instant-gratification kitchen project. Good things, however, come to those who wait. Breathe. Slow down a little. We love you.

What Is Fermentation?

Quick pickling is when you simply use a vinegar brine to get your fruits and veggies into their pickle suits. Fermentation, however, takes its sweet time. Although it doesn't sound very appetizing, fermentation is essentially controlled rot.

When you ferment foods and drinks, you prep tasty whole foods—fruits, vegetables, beans and legumes, nuts and seeds, etc.—and then set up the proper conditions for microorganisms to break them down and transform them into something that's usually significantly more delicious and nutritious than what you

I Don't Know What I'm Doing

I made kvass for the first time a couple years ago. If you don't know what it is, it's a very low-alcohol Slavic and Baltic fermented drink made with rye bread. Had I ever had it before? No. Had I ever watched someone make it? Nope. Why did I decide to make kvass, you ask? A lot of the foods and drinks I make have a very simple motivation: I want to try something new. I want to learn something and get my hands in it. The really important and, I think, cool thing is that a lot of the time, I mess things up. I think you should too.

I made the kvass, drank a little, and thought, This isn't very good. There was too much residual sugar, the ABV (alcohol by volume) was too high, and the flavor was off. I took it to Bonnie Morales, chef-owner of the Portland Russian restaurant Kachka. She drank a little and said, "This isn't very good." She was right; it sucked. And that was OK. It simply meant I had more work to do.

If you want to understand how to be a successful person in any field, you shouldn't be afraid of fucking up. And when you do fuck up, learn a lesson or two from it. If you go about life paralyzed by fear, then you're not going to go anywhere. That isn't to say I'm never afraid—heck no, I'm often terrified. I just don't let it stop me.

started with. Sometimes the process is a bit slow (hello, Chickpea Miso, page 61, and Wine-Washed Aged Cheese, page 141), and sometimes it's superfast (hey, Ginger Beer, page 113, and Pickle Kraut, page 47). An added bonus is the historic thousands-of-years-old intent: ferments are heaps more shelf stable than their raw and fresh former selves.

Building a Ferment

You know that real estate saying "Location, location, location"? Fellow fermenters, please repeat after me: "Conditions, conditions, conditions." If you create the ideal conditions for bacteria, yeasts, molds, etc. to thrive throughout the fermentation process, you're well on your way to future deliciousness. Ingredients matter too, of course—heck yes they do—but most importantly you want to make your environment as hospitable as possible to all the microorganisms. These are the superstars who will work their asses off to turn your raw veggies, fruits, legumes, grains, etc. into yummy, next-level things.

LAB Ferments

Most folks dipping their toes into fermentation start with LAB ferments—krauts, sour pickles, fermented hot sauces—to name a few. The first six recipes in this book, in fact, are all LAB ferments, meaning they have lactic acid bacteria, a.k.a. *Lactobacillus*, which is on the surface of just about everything, to thank for their tasty fermentation transformation. If you want to sound like a pro, go ahead and shorten lactic acid bacteria ferments to LAB ferments like the cool kids do.

Below the Brine

The old pickling and fermenting adage, "Below the brine and it'll be fine," is spot-on. Please follow that advice when making our Sour Dills & Pickle Brine (page 39), Hot Behind Hot Sauce (page 41), North Coast Kraut (page 45), and any of our other lacto-bacteria veggie ferments.

The reason why you want to keep these fermenting veggies under the brine is because they're anaerobic, the opposite of aerobic. That means, as they ferment, they don't want to come into contact with very much air. If they do, less desirable microorganisms often barrel through the door—ones that cause surface molds and yeasts, like the ubiquitous kahm yeast (see What the Heck Is Kahm Yeast, Anyway?, page 11). The end result of these little jerks crashing your fermentation party is, more often than not, off-flavors and textures. It's not the end of the world, but it's definitely not desirable, and it's generally very much avoidable.

Have Controls or Lose Control

Don't change everything all at once from one batch of a ferment to the next. Be like a lab-coated scientist, and make only one small change or two each time you make the thing. That way, you'll know much better what worked and what didn't. You believe in science, right?

With tempeh (pages 77–95), for instance, I highly recommend that once you find a bean, legume, or bean, legume, and grain mix that works for you, make tempeh with that over and over, until you get it just right, and then you'll really learn tempeh. If you're constantly changing your substrate (the medium in which the reaction takes place, your beans/legumes/grains), it'll be difficult to understand how things should progress time-wise, smell-wise, taste-wise.

I started with 100 percent black bean tempeh. I'm guessing I made black bean tempeh nearly 50 times before I finally moved on to other combos of beans, legumes, and grains. That was my tempeh school. I graduated.

While I'm at it, please start with relatively traditional ferments before you go nuts. How many cooks have I met that have made super-complicated, oh, I don't know, possum paw garums, but never a simple soybean miso? Well, none, but you get what I mean. Use and learn from the map, and at least get the lay of the land before you chuck it out the window. Also, don't litter.

USE WHAT YOU HAVE
FOR A FERMENT VESSEL
AND SCRUB-A-DUB IT
WITH HOT, SOAPY WATER
PRE-USE

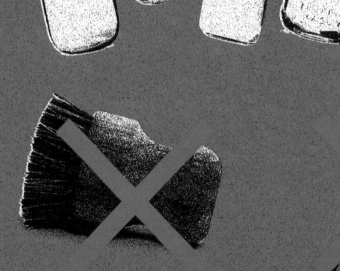

DON'T SCRUB YOUR
VEG TO DEATH

LEAVE THE VEG
BIRTHDAY SUIT ON FOR
YOUR LACTIC PARTY

TOP YOUR FERMENT
WITH BREATHABLE
CLOTH AND SECURE
IT WITH TWINE OR A
RUBBER BAND

KEEP YOUR FERMENTS OUT
OF DIRECT SUNLIGHT

USE FILTERED WATER

Organic, Please

Fungicides, herbicides, and pesticides can adversely affect your ferments. It's best for the planet, as well as the success of your ferments, to use organic. Please do. Chemicals kill microbes.

Let's say you don't use organic beans, legumes, and grains for our various tempehs (pages 77–95). The short and not-so-sweet of it is, you might end up with spotty *Rhizopus* growth (page 95) throughout, even if you follow every step of our recipe to the letter. If those guys making up the substrate of your tempeh have been born and bred on fungicides, well, how much of a chance does the *Rhizopus* really have? *Rhizopus oligosporus* and *Rhizopus oryzae*, by the way, are the good guys, the BFFs of tempeh. They are the common fungi that make tempeh, well, tempeh. When *Rhizopus* is perfectly bloomed, on the surface of and throughout the tempeh, it looks like a white fluffy blanketing of snow.

Daily Check-Ins

You don't have to check on most actively fermenting ferments daily: some can go for weeks to months A-OK like a hermit (I'm looking at you, Chickpea Miso, page 61), with no outside interactions. But I think you should bug them a bit, at least while you're learning the ropes. By doing so, you'll keep things like kahm yeast and other icky molds and bacteria at bay, and you'll also get a better idea of the whole process and the day-to-day and week-to-week transformation. Also, please taste-test when you do check in. Don't forget to feed the fermenter!

Stay on the Dark Side. Maybe . . .

You know how people are always saying how important it is to keep ferments in the dark and out of direct sunlight? Are ferments vampiric? No, many of them include hearty amounts of garlic! Are they shy? Most are fairly bold, actually. So what's the deal?

Actually, I'm just not sure. I don't believe direct sunlight, other than possibly increasing the heat of my crock, will be all that harmful to lactic acid bacteria ferments.

There's a lot of contradictory information on whether light is beneficial or harmful to yeasts used in fermentation. Some say sunlight can cause yeast overgrowth, while others say sunlight kills yeast. One thing is for sure, when you ferment out of direct sunlight, you stand less of a chance of overheating your ferment.

It's traditional to keep many ferments out of direct sunlight. Maybe that's enough of a good reason? I'm guessing that most seasoned old-timey makers had really high-quality ferments in their cellars. They were reliant upon them, so they weren't fucking around. Who are we to argue with thousands of years of expertise and anecdotal evidence?

Of course, there are tons of exceptions. Please go with your gut and try stuff out. Maybe make two small jars of the same ferment, and hide one in a dark closet and put the other on a south-facing windowsill (if you're in the Northern Hemisphere) and find out. Keep me posted.

Tare It Up! A.k.a. Making Brine by Using a Scale

In a lot of the recipes in Part 1 of the book, you'll see both a recommended salt volume and a salt-by-weight percentage in the ingredient list. Adding salt as a percentage of the ferment's overall weight is a more precise way to salt your ferments, and it's how we do it at Fermenter. You'll obviously need a kitchen scale (page 27).

In most of the recipes, we ask you to add either 2 to 2.5 percent salt or 5 percent salt. Don't worry—we always include volume as well. A scale can be a really reliable kitchen friend, though, because it allows you to be much more precise.

Tare it up! Turn on your kitchen scale, and set it to grams rather than ounces. Place the clean vessel that you'll be fermenting in onto your kitchen scale, and tare the scale—in other words, reset the weight to 0 grams. Once tared, leave the vessel on the scale and add all the ingredients that you'll be fermenting, except for salt, and including water if you're using it.

Once you've added all the recipe's ingredients, including water if it's called for, take the total number of grams designated on the scale and multiply that number by the percentage of salt called for in the recipe. If the recipe calls for 2 to 2.5 percent salt, then multiply the number of grams respectively by either 0.02 or 0.025. If the recipe calls for 5 percent salt, then multiply the number of grams by 0.05. The resulting number is the weight in grams of salt called for in the recipe. So go ahead and weigh out that amount of salt and then add it to your ferment. Easy!

Keep It Clean

Wash your hands and forearms with hot, soapy water before you start a new ferment. Scrub under your fingernails! If you don't feel like scrub-a-dub-dubbing, then slap on some vinyl or nitrile gloves.

Treat your fermenting vessels—jars, crocks, jugs, buckets, whatever—the same way. Clean or sanitize them properly. We wash ours with hot, soapy water at Fermenter, and after that we spray them with a 50/50 vinegar-plus-water solution. Use any vinegar, as long as it's at least 5 percent acidic, which means it has a pH of 2.4 or less. Distilled white, apple cider, and white wine vinegars are all great and are typically in this range. Air-dry your sanitized fermentation vessel and then get fermenting.

BUILDING A LACTIC ACID

1

2

3

4

1   Clean your fermentation vessel.

2   Slice or chop your veggies.

3   Salt them.

4   Pack your fermentation vessel.

BACTERIA (LAB) FERMENT

5

6

7

8

5   Wipe inside headspace of jar.

6   Top the salted vegetables with your preferred follower.

7   Top the follower with your preferred weight.

8   Secure the whole shebang with breathable cloth.

Backslop Might Sound Gross but . . .

It's a beautiful thing. And it's another option if your ferment isn't juicy enough or simply needs a little jump start. You can always add some backslop—a.k.a. mature pickle brine, kraut juice, kombucha (a.k.a. booch), vinegar, etc.—from another finished ferment to a just-started ferment. That's not to say you should dump old kombucha into your sauerkraut. Keep your culture sets within the family!

At Fermenter, we always save our pickle brine for this purpose. We usually have a couple dozen gallons of it in the walk-in at any given point. And we're whey (groan) into saving our whey as well, to jump-start ferments and culture things.

Adding backslop doesn't just add moisture in order to submerge things; it also adds flavor. As well, it gives just-started ferments a bit of a boost in the form of an already developed culture set—a little extra help in the tasty transformation from the get-go.

If you don't add backslop or brine to a dry kraut, for instance, in order to submerge the sliced cabbage, you'll likely get some surface mold and yuckity yuck on top. Once you're done fermenting and you refrigerate your kraut, it also often seizes up and pulls in moisture as it chills. Go ahead and pour in some brine when it does.

So try to always have a bit of brine on hand—loaded up with 2 to 2.5 percent salt (page 7). It's best if the brine is drawn off from a previous batch of kraut, pickles, etc., but in a pinch, filtered water plus 2 to 2.5 percent salt by weight does the trick. You won't need it when a ferment is really juicy, but sometimes you'll reach for it to top things off. Keep it juicy!

Burp Your Babies

Even once you think your ferment is at its prime, and you've packed it up and tucked it into your refrigerator to chill, it still needs some TLC. The transformation has slowed way down to a creep, in terms of fermenting, but it's still kicking. It's very much alive.

So every once in a while, if you aren't using a jarred or bottled ferment in the fridge regularly, be a sweetheart and check on it. It's a good idea to burp—a.k.a. open up and off-gas—your ferments every now and again. They can build up significant pressure and also start to separate due to continued, albeit slow, fermentation. Spoon up any icky surface stuff, wipe down the headspace with a clean rag, and then give them a hearty shake or stir so that undesirable surface yeasts and molds don't take over. If you're checking on brined ferments, make sure that everything is below the brine (see Below the Brine, page 3) for the long haul.

Test the Water

You don't have to use filtered water for your brines and ferments, but if you have a lot of trace metals, contaminants, and chlorine in your water, they won't do you any favors. Chlorine is also antimicrobial. When you use chlorinated water without filtering, evaporating, or boiling it, you'll end up with more yeasts in your final products. The taste will most likely be a bit off too.

All you need is a Brita pitcher, or something cheap, to remove a good deal of contaminants and chlorine, although you can do better. My wife, Jenny, and I have a Berkey filter at home, but it's expensive and a bit slow. At Fermenter, we have a large commercial filter that produces fairly pristine water. Luckily, Portland water straight from the reservoir is pretty darn good already.

If you don't want to filter your water, that's your prerogative. At the very least though, if you have chlorinated water, pull what you need from the tap before you're going to use it, cover it with a towel, and let it sit for 24 hours and up to five days to evaporate the chlorine. You can speed things up by boiling your water for 15 minutes. After it's boiled, cover it with a towel, and cool it to room temperature.

If you don't believe me, here's a test. Take 1,000 grams of unfiltered water and 1,000 grams of filtered water from the same tap. Reduce them down to 200 grams each by simmering them. Let them cool, then pour each of them into a different wineglass. The filtered water will most likely be clear, and the unfiltered water will be piss yellow. So? Go for the non-piss-yellow situation.

What the Heck Is Kahm Yeast, Anyway?

If you've got a whitish film growing on the top of your ferment and/or a significant cloudiness in your ferment, don't despair—it's most likely kahm yeast. It's ubiquitous. Kahm yeast is a surface mold that ranges from spotty and cloudy to thicker and crepe-paper-like or velvety. Just know this: you're not failing if it shows up. We all get it from time to time. It's relatively harmless beyond the fact that it can develop some off-flavors and textures in your ferments if it takes over. Simply scoop, scrape, or towel it off the top, and wipe down your vessel. Keep away kahm and carry on.

Size Matters

We really want you to feel comfortable increasing and reducing yields throughout the book, and we want you to know that size matters, particularly with ferments. When scaling up, in general, be aware that your fermentation time will take a bit longer if you're working with a SCOBY (symbiotic culture of bacteria and yeast, a.k.a. a "mother") or another culture set (vinegars, kombuchas, water kefirs), and it will take a bit less time if you scale up on things that generate significant heat (tempehs and koji). For instance, at Fermenter, our big 30-gallon batches of kombucha take about two weeks to a month to ferment, depending on the time of year. At home, this book's 1 gallon–batch kombuchas will typically take you a week or less.

Don't Use a Veggie Wash!

Although you do want to rinse your veggies before fermenting them, please don't use any of those commercial veggie washes or grapefruit seed extracts on them. If you do, you'll lose some of the awesome, diverse microbial life on the surface. Don't scrub the shit out of them!

Toast Your Spices

The chef in me almost always wants to toast whole dried spices and sometimes dried herbs too. When you do so, you activate them a bit and bring out their volatile oils and flavor compounds. When you're fermenting, toasting dried herbs and spices gives you the added bonus of knocking out any lingering pathogens that may be living on the surface. For me, I'm all about the flavor that toasting brings out, and I really don't worry too much about pathogens. Some people do though, and if you do, this will hopefully help you sleep a little bit better at night. Sleep is good.

Since we aren't including toasting notes in each recipe, here's the gist: Put your small to large (depending on the batch size of your ferment) dry skillet over medium heat—don't add any oil or fat! Once the pan is hot, add your herbs and spices to it, and basically just toss or move them around in the pan for roughly 2 to 4 minutes. You want to toast them until your kitchen starts to smell aromatic and the spices and herbs have darkened a bit. Some might even start popping. Don't walk away! You've got to keep everything moving around in the pan so that you toast rather than burn them.

Once everything is nicely toasted, transfer the herbs and spices to a cool plate or pan. I like to throw a little quarter baking sheet into the cooler at Fermenter for an hour or so before I toast my spices. When they're done, I pull the sheet out and cool them on it. That stops their cooking immediately. We do huge batches of things at Fermenter, though. For you, a fridge-chilled bowl or plate will work just fine for most recipes in the book.

Good Things Take Time

There are some recipes in this book that will definitely surprise you in terms of the sheer number of steps involved and the time required to complete them. I'm thinking primarily of Part 1 of the book: the ferments. Maybe your grams or gramps told you at some point, "Good things take time, kiddo." Well, it turns out they're right. And *you're* also right if you don't want to allot, oh, I don't know, say the better part of a week to make some of our tasty beets (Koji Beets, page 73). They're so good, though!

The thing is, imagine making all of our more complicated ferments (Tempeh Bacon, page 88; Wine-Washed Aged Cheese, page 141; Shio Koji, page 70) in your comfy home on your time, in a small yield, on your days off. (You look great, by the way. Nice houseplants. Cool apron!) OK, then imagine us making those ferments, week after week, in our not-palatial restaurant—checking in on them, monitoring all the various conditions—while also slinging plant-based meals, right and left, for all our favorite people in the fine city of Portland. It's a lot. And it's worth it! For us. You get to try it all out at your own pace and scale and see.

And maybe, if you don't decide, after cooking from this book, to DIY each and every one of your tempeh, miso, yogurt, kombucha, kefir, and vinegar needs, you'll appreciate all the plant-based artisans doing these delicious things day in and day out just a little bit more. Those rad plant-based cheesemakers, artisan tempeh makers, and expert miso makers all sure do deserve your respect and appreciation. Maybe you'll make them a dope gallon of one of our booches now as a thank-you. Our booches (pages 107-112) are so easy to make!

Community

You can be a hermit and make tasty ferments, for sure. But you won't enjoy them as much, and when you make a big batch of kraut, pickles, hot sauce, etc., you're going to get pretty dang sick of eating them by the time you're at the bottom of the barrel. Ferment your veggies, and ferment your community. Then you can share and trade ferments and all those fermentation lessons learned. Make fermentation friends—at your local co-op, farmers' market, hippie supply store. Wherever. Do it.

And, I don't know, maybe start a fermentation festival in your town if there isn't one already. My coauthor, Liz, started one in Portland with friends in 2009— the annual Portland Fermentation Festival—and that's how a lot of us Portland fermentation folks know each other. It's also one reason why we've gotten our hero, Sandor Ellix Katz, to keep coming back to our fair city year after year, along with a lot of wonderful fermenters from Japan, as well as David Zilber formerly from Noma in Copenhagen.

Community is key. The number of alliances and friendships that I've grown over the years in the wide world of fermentation is astounding to me. When I sit down and start to make a list, it just keeps going and going. The beauty of it is, there's all sorts of cross-pollination. We all share ideas, ingredients, knowledge, supplies, equipment. It's special. Folks like my bud Eytan Zias of Portland Knife House, Earnest and Yuri Migaki of Jorinji Miso, Jordyn Bunting of Oregon State University's Food Innovation Center, Sarah Pesout of the Fermentista, Humiko Hozumi and Jason Duffany of Obon Shokudo, Karen McAthy of Blue Heron Creamery. So many beautiful people.

History Is Punk

While I want to tell you that Fermenter was a dream of mine for many years while working my ass off in fine dining, the truth is, it started off as a fuck-you to a landlord. I had a small space that we rented and ran Farm Spirit (my 14-seat fine dining, chef's counter vegan restaurant) out of for a while, and then we wanted a bigger space. We moved a block away but kept the original spot because the rent was so dang cheap. We used that original space as a workshop studio for fermentation projects and pastry work because it had a good oven.

After we'd been cruising with that MO for a while, the landlord said, "Hey, you need to have something here, you can't just have a blank space. You need to have something that's open to the public." So I said, "Fine, whatever." I put four seats in the front, added a tiny counter, and said, "OK, it's Fermenter." I called it that and had a fuck-all Fermenter heavy-metal logo made. I didn't care, I was just doing it to appease the landlord. I had no intention of it really being a thing.

While I was working at Farm Spirit, I thought, *Why don't we do a three-course lunch over there at Fermenter?* Just try it out. And you know what? People liked it. So we decided to work on it, and it went from there.

Then the pandemic hit. Farm Spirit was running in one spot, and Fermenter was open just a block away in that small original space. In those early days of the pandemic, we didn't know what to do. No one did. We kind of combined forces and did a Farm Spirit plus Fermenter mash-up dinner for a bit—a boxed-food sort of thing that people picked up as a meal kit. And then we eventually opened up for dining with another Fermenter/Farm Spirit mash-up. But we all just felt bad about doing service in the middle of the pandemic, so we went ahead and shut Farm Spirit down completely. Chef counter-service and multicourse fine dining didn't really jibe with the plague, you know?

I built out an ordering counter in the old and larger Farm Spirit space, and we opened it up again. This time as Fermenter. Once and for all. So be careful with what you do in a fuck-all frenzy because you never know, it might just become your main gig.

"WILL I DIE IF I EAT IT?" & OTHER FAQS

Do you hate me if I'm not 100 percent vegan?

Every night I say to my wife, "I love you, Jenny, but I also hate you because you're not vegan." No! That's not true. Of course I don't hate you. And I don't hate my wife! I don't hate you if you're 0 percent vegan. I don't cast judgment on anyone's dietary choices. If you caught me 20 years ago, though, I would have been like, "Fuck you! If you aren't vegan, then you don't care about anything!"

When we look at the gift and punishment of the human perception of time—it seems so slow, but relative to what's going on in the universe, the billions of years that came before us, the billions of years that will come after—none of the shit that we do matters all that much. So who cares? Half-joking aside, what feels good to me, at this point in my life, is to do as little harm to the planet as I can while I'm here, and that includes eating and cooking vegan. That makes sense to me, but if you don't feel it, you don't feel it. And I get that.

There's a huge historical, momentous force that informs us and pushes us to eat animals and to live and act a certain way—the CAFO meat (a.k.a. concentrated animal feeding operation, a.k.a. a cruel, inhumane, and awful-for-the-environment nightmare), industrial food and farms way. It's really hard to slow that train down. So in the words of Bill Murray, in that sweet 1979 movie *Meatballs*, "It just doesn't matter." Please enjoy the material pleasures of life, to the best of your ability.

Until we all perish and enter the void.

What are the easiest ferments to start with in this book, and which are most difficult for a newbie fermenter? I want easy.

I'd say that the easiest ferments to start with are the lactic acid bacteria ones, which are primarily in Eat Your Salty, Sour Vegetables! (pages 36–55). The most difficult recipes are mostly in the Mold Is Gold chapter (pages 58–95)—the bean, legume, and rice ferments like tempeh and koji. You can do all of it. I believe in you!

What if I forget about one of your ferments in the back of the fridge, and it's been in there longer than you say it should be—will I die if I eat it?

We give you "good until" times for most of the recipes, ranging from days to months, but the truth is, a lot of these ferments keep just about indefinitely. Those time frames are simply for when they are at their best. We don't keep things all that long at Fermenter because we're busy as all get-out, and we don't stockpile because, in general, we favor fresh. We also just don't have the room to store them.

At home you most likely can and will keep things longer. That's great. Please don't worry about it. I'd say the biggest thing you'll want to look out for is significant texture deterioration. Some ferments can get pretty soft and yucky after a while.

In general, the nose knows. Use your senses. Organoleptic all the way. Does it smell good, look good, feel good? If it's not stinky bad, nasty looking, slimy in a bad way, gross, etc., chances are it's perfectly fine to eat or drink up. Unless someone is out to get you and slipped some undetectable poison in there, which happens, so watch out.

And just so you know, I have a separate fridge out in my garage at home that's entirely mine. (Basically, my wife, Jenny, got really sick of our perpetually crowded-with-ferments fridge, and I panicked.) It's filled to the gills with ferments from all over the place. Some of those ferments have been in there way longer than any sort of sell-by date.

What are your feelings about substitutions and variations?

I really, really hope that you'll be inspired by my recipes while also utilizing your own intelligence and intuition. For instance, if you're short on this, that, or the other ingredient, you're probably going to be just fine substituting something similar. In terms of cultures, spores, and SCOBYs (see Ingredients, page 19), though, please use the ones we recommend unless you're comfortable gambling on the desired results.

Can I speed up any of these ferments? Patience isn't exactly my thing.

You can always try cranking up the heat a little bit to speed things up. You'll probably sacrifice some texture, you might create some off-flavors, and you might foster some undesirable yeast growth, but have at it, Speedy.

When it comes to lactic acid fermentation or brewing kombucha or kefir, you don't want to up the heat too terribly much because the conditions you create, based on the instructions throughout our recipes, will deliver what we deem the most desirable results. If you blaze a path and set up conditions that are different, well, you'll most likely get different results.

If you're fermenting vinegars, there are some methods and techniques out there to speed things up. Go get an aquarium bubbler and go to town aerating your vinegar. Or sit over it and stir it constantly like a lunatic. You do you. All of that said, if patience isn't your thing, maybe start with something fairly quick and easy, like our Ruby Kraut recipe on page 51. No shame.

Can I can any of the ferments in the book? Also, do you know how to can-can?

I'm not a Master Food Preserver. Meaning, I'm not giving you the ins and outs for water-bath canning or pressure canning any of the ferments here. If you want to can them, then you'll need to properly educate yourself and hopefully consult a Master Food Preserver. That's a fun thing to do. You can usually find them by contacting your local university agricultural extension office or by visiting their website. I don't want you to get the botulism and die, so I'm not giving you canning steps. I also don't want you to throw this book at me, so I'm not going to don my frilly petticoat and can-can for you.

Does kombucha contain alcohol?

The cool thing about kombucha, versus vinegar, is that while they both produce acetic acid, as well as some other acids, vinegar is a two-step process. Alcohol is first produced and then converted into acetic acid. In kombucha, both alcohol and acetic acid are created at the same time.

Acetic acid is the fermentation by-product that gives vinegar and kombucha, and many other foods and drinks, their big bright tang. Basically, the microscopic acetic acid bacteria get hungry and busy, and while they boogie around doing their thing with your tea that will become kombucha, and your boozy juice that will become vinegar, they produce sour funky acetic acid that makes everything taste so dang good.

Acetic acid transformation happens with the help of airflow and oxygen. If you brew your kombucha with an airlock, so that there's no airflow, you'll most likely end up with a higher ABV and less-acidic kombucha than if you simply cover it in cloth. The less you aerate your kombucha, the more alcohol it will contain.

It's a personal choice in terms of booch alcohol content, of course. I know plenty of people who are sober who drink kombucha, and plenty of people who are sober who don't. Most of our kombuchas at Fermenter are right around 0.5 percent ABV—super low, about the same as a day-old glass of orange juice.

Can I make a salt-free ferment?

Salt is great because it inhibits pathogenic bacteria, and it also prevents texture deterioration. So although you don't have to use salt, it's advisable. If possible, you should simply use less of it. Your saltless ferment might not be dangerous, but it might not be delicious either. And it might give you and your loved ones a tummy ache.

Is lactic acid vegan?

I think that since the words *lactic* and *lactose* look and sound so similar, a lot of people get confused and think *lactic* must be directly related to milk and lactose, right? Please rest assured that although it can be produced from dairy products, as well as from meat and seafood, the lactic acid produced in veggie ferments is 100 percent vegan.

Can I cultivate my own koji and tempeh spores?

Please don't. Koji is a domesticated form of wild *Aspergillus*, a genus of various mold species, which is toxic. There's a possibility of a mutation with every growth of spores. That means those spores of yours can just as easily mutate into something that straight up won't be good for you. Yes, ancient people cultivated koji with success, but they did it with intense and prolonged studying and observation, so unless you have a testing laboratory, please refrain.

I just think that with us watching all those darn TikToks, most of us don't have the time required to observe the subtle differences in koji and tempeh spores in order to safely and properly cultivate them. Also, hey, they're freaking inexpensive! I know I stress DIY, but in this case, DDIY: don't do it.

INGREDIENTS

Beans, Legumes, and Grains

Local beans, legumes, and grains are where it's at, so please try to find out which ones grow well in your neck of the woods and source them.

Methylcellulose HV

To make our vegan sausages, you'll need to get your hands on methylcellulose HV (high viscosity). You can find it online at places like Modernist Pantry. This is a really unusual ingredient for us because it's not local or natural. It's 100 percent laboratory created. That said, it allows us to present our sausage in a way that's novel and interesting. And it makes people eat more tempeh!

Nuts

We love local, and we love Oregon hazelnuts, a.k.a. filberts. They're a huge crop here and a big point of pride for Oregonians. So get some if you can.

Oils and Butters

High-oleic sunflower oil is our preferred go-to cooking oil at Fermenter, but feel free to sub other neutral oils. Generic vegetable oil is usually pretty terrible, and canola oil is so political that we just avoid it altogether.

For vegan butter, we highly recommend Flora, if you can find it, but we also like Miyoko's Creamery cultured vegan butter. Miyoko's is the best quality and flavor, but we like Flora for a balance of performance and price. Earth Balance is fine if you can't find either of those two.

Produce

When it comes to parsley, it's always flat-leaf parsley and never curly for us. Really, curly parsley is fine—it's just been so smashed into our heads, those of us who've spent years in professional kitchens, that flat-leaf is the way and the truth, so I can't use curly parsley anymore. I'm damaged goods. You do what you like.

We source a lot of our herbs and spices from Mountain Rose Herbs (page 216) in Eugene, Oregon. They're all about organic and sustainable, and all the other good stuff. They do online orders and ship anywhere.

Salt

We generally stick to fine sea salt for our ferments—it dissolves quickly and easily and tastes good—and kosher salt otherwise. My wife, Jenny, and I use Jacobsen Salt Co. salts at home and we use Giusto's Natural Sea Salt at the restaurant. Feel free to use whatever the heck kind of salt you want. Just be aware that moisture levels and texture greatly influence weight: you'll want to use a little less in volume when substituting a finer and moister salt, and a bit more in volume for a drier, coarser salt. Of course, a fairly accurate way to measure salt content is to just taste it. Duh.

SCOBYs

Kombucha SCOBYs are pretty dang easy to source. First, if you have a friend DIYing homemade booch, go ahead and ask them for a SCOBY. Since kombucha SCOBYs grow and reproduce constantly (bunnies come to mind), and jars and crocks to contain them are only so big, you'll actually be doing them a favor by taking a SCOBY off their hands. Don't know anyone homebrewing booch? Purchase a SCOBY at your local food cooperative, homebrew supply shop, or DIY or hippie supply shop selling things like cheesecloth and water-bath canners. If you've got none of that, buy one online at a rad business like Cultures for Health (page 215) or Kombucha Kamp (page 216).

Spores and Cultures

Look, there are all sorts of great sources for fermentation spores and cultures, and as with everything in life, diversity is key. That said, we've had some bummer ones over the years, so here's a short list of ones we give our seal of approval to (for more details, see Resources on pages 215-216). Bio'c Co. koji spores are great but can be hard for the average consumer to get directly. We also love using koji spores from GEM Cultures. For tempeh, look to Raprima: you can order small amounts from them, shipped straight from Indonesia. We like vegan cheese cultures from The Cheesemaker, though we're anxiously awaiting the cheese cultures soon to be released by our friend Karen McAthy, a Canadian chef and founder of Blue Heron Creamery. For a lot of other stuff, Cultures for Health online is great!

Sugar

Sugar is always organic pure cane sugar throughout the book unless noted otherwise.

Tea

Please always opt for quality tea for your kombuchas. We love using and working with Steven Smith because it is an exceptional local teamaker in Portland, but please source your tea from your favorite local(ish) teamaker.

Vegan Yogurt Culture

If you have a local cheesemaking shop, or any DIY or hippie supply shop, you might find this there. If not, there are heaps of online options. Most vegan yogurt packets contain enough culture for several batches of our Sunflower Yogurt (page 130).

Water

Filtered water (see Test the Water, page 10) is the way to go when it comes to adding water to your ferments and, we'll go so far as to say, when it comes to adding water to anything you consume. When water is included in our recipes, we recommend filtered.

Xanthan Gum

Xanthan gum is a plant-based food thickener and emulsifier that's often used in GF baking (thickens!) or sauces (thickens *and* emulsifies!). You'll find it in most grocery store baking aisles. It's a fine white powder and a little goes a long way, so please add it incrementally.

When using it for our hot sauce (page 41), blend the xanthan gum right into the vortex of the sauce, with the blender running. Incrementally add up to ⅛ teaspoon, although probably just a pinch in total. Blend until the sauce (or whatever else you want to thicken) is the thick, smooth consistency you want.

If your xanthan gum is particularly clumpy, make a gel and refrigerate it for up to 2 months. To make the gel: In the bowl of your blender, blend 1 cup of cold water plus 1 teaspoon of xanthan gum on high speed for 3 minutes. Add up to 1 to 2 tablespoons of the resulting gel to the sauce, blending for 3 to 4 more minutes, and carry on with the recipe.

EQUIPMENT

Over the past couple of years I've taught a lot of fermentation classes. At some point during almost every class, I'll get one or two people asking nervously about fermentation equipment—what they have versus what they worry they'll need.

I'm here to put your mind at ease. It's all pretty simple. Beyond a jar or crock, a knife, and a cutting board, you really don't need much to get going in the wide world of fermentation. That said, I think the following items will most likely make the whole endeavor easier and more enjoyable.

Brød & Taylor Folding Proofer & Slow Cooker

We love this proofer, especially for incubating koji. Basically, when it comes to fermentation, a proofer allows you to keep an exact temperature (often quite low, lower than your oven), for the desired amount of time with somewhat controlled humidity. At around $200, this one isn't cheap, but if you want to make a sound investment and make things easy on yourself, you can use it for so many things in this book. It will be your BFF when you make our Pinto Bean Tempeh (page 85), Tempeh Burger Patties

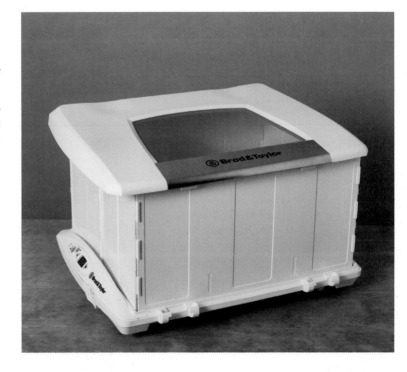

FINE-MESH SIEVE

CHEESE PAPER

1-GALLON PORCELAIN CROCK

FLIP-TOP BOTTLES

MUSLIN, A.K.A. BREATHABLE CLOTH

FLIP-TOP CANNING JAR

THERMOMETER

KOJI SPORE SHAKER

POUNDER, A.K.A. KRAUT CRUSHER

3-GALLON STONEWARE CROCK

KOJI TRAY

FERMENTATION WEIGHTS

SHARP KNIFE

(page 91), Koji Rice (page 63), Koji Beets (page 73), Sunflower Yogurt (page 130), and more. And you can use it for all sorts of other cool kitchen projects—bread proofing, obviously; slow cooking; and even as a warming plate for parties. It folds up nicely, so it never gets in the way. We love it. Don't worry: we also give you info on DIYing home fermentation/incubation chambers (see Incubating, page 80).

Cheese Paper

If you don't have cheese paper and you're planning to make the book's plant-based cheeses (pages 133–147), please get some. It'll aid in both making cheese (you age it on the paper) and storing it. Cheese paper is two things at once—it's breathable and seals in moisture. It's two-ply: generally the inner paper is waxed, and the outer paper is a low-density shinier polyethylene. Cheese needs to breathe, and if it's stored in cheese paper, versus plastic wrap, it will keep about three times longer. Cheese is sensitive, just like you and me.

Fermentation Weights

There are so many ways you can go with ferment weights—from a super-simple plastic bag filled with brine to a combination of plastic wrap and then stone, glass, or ceramic weights. Basically, you just want something durable that will keep your fermentables (cucumbers, cabbage, chilies, etc.) submerged below the brine and/or somewhat shielded from air.

A brine-filled bag serves two purposes: it weighs down the ferment, and it seals all the surface gaps of the vessel. The point is to keep air out and prohibit airborne molds from entering. For small-volume ferments in jars, we like brine-filled bags.

For larger-vessel and longer-duration ferments in crocks and buckets, we like river stones. Our friends at The Cultured Pickle Shop (page 215) turned us on to them. Give them a good scrub, of course, and make sure they are super-duper clean before using them. Then place each one in a large plastic bag and set them on top of your ferment.

Followers

In the world of fermentation, a follower is simply something that directly covers your ferments. The primary follower is typically whatever weight or weights you use to keep your ferment submerged. It can also be a cabbage leaf, grape leaf, or whatever else you get creative with.

For our ferments, we usually start with a plastic wrap primary follower that sits directly on the surface of the ferment, followed by fermentation weights (which we also usually wrap in plastic wrap), followed by a thin, breathable cloth over the top of the fermentation vessel. We don't use very much plastic wrap at Fermenter, but it's really helpful as a primary follower, because it allows us to see what's going on down below in the dozens of ferments that we typically have going at any given time. Don't be a follower, but please use them!

Hydrometer

You'll only potentially need this piece of brewing equipment (get them for $10 to $30 at a brew supply shop) for one recipe in the book—Apple Cider Vinegar (page 100), and that's only if you fresh-press the cider for it. If you use store-bought apple cider, the sugar content will be high enough already and good to go. If you press your own apple cider, you'll want to weigh the density of it, a.k.a. the gravity/sugar content, with a hydrometer. Then you will add more sugar to it if there isn't enough. I don't have any particular allegiances when it comes to hydrometer type or brand.

Instant-Read Thermometers

There are so many recipes in this book that require temperature readings—including the Pinto Bean Tempeh (page 85), Tempeh Burger Patties (page 91), Sunflower Yogurt (page 130), Koji Beets (page 73), etc.—that, by golly, if you don't have one already, I highly recommend getting a good instant-read thermometer or two. The price range widely varies here, and in general, you do get what you pay for. Thermapens, for instance, are super fast, reliable, and well made, *and* most are in the $100 range. If you can spare a Benjamin Franklin, get one. Other so-called instant-read thermometers may be a heck of a lot cheaper, but will be less reliable, and generally take several seconds to get a good reading. A probe thermometer, the kind a lot of pit and barbecue folks use, can be super handy too for leaving inserted in things for continuous temperature monitoring.

Kitchen Scales

Get one if you don't have one: they're cheap, and they allow you to be more precise with your ferments when you want to be. Escali is a good brand. I don't really feel like pushing a brand here, though. In our kitchen, we use a hefty platform scale, because we're often weighing 40 to 60 pounds of kraut at a time. Don't store stuff on top of your scale, and try not to grab it by the top. Cooking nerds like to buy calibration weights for their scales, but just use whatever thing you've got around that you're certain about the weight of. Your hamster?

Kojibutas, Morobutas & Kojibans—a.k.a. Koji Trays

These are all different words for the same thing: a rectangular cedar tray that you inoculate and culture koji on. The first two words are what they're often called in Japan, and the third is what folks in the United States often call them. They're usually handmade by artisans, and the cedar and their shape help regulate moisture levels and temperature. They make such a difference in terms of incubating quality koji. At

Fermenter, we carry American white cedar ones custom-made for us by Quercus Cooperage in New York that fit perfectly inside the Brød & Taylor folding proofer (page 23).

Koji Spore Shaker

Koji spores are so light and fine that we find they need their own special gadget for inoculating our Koji Rice (page 63), Koji Beets (page 73), and any other things we use them for. Basically, get a small powdered-sugar shaker and then situate one or two layers of cheesecloth beneath the fine-mesh topper. This combination of the mesh and cheesecloth allows you to evenly dust and apply the koji spores.

pH Strips or a pH Meter

You can definitely get by without pH strips or a pH meter, but if you're making a lot of ferments (and you want to geek out), I highly recommend getting one or the other (you can get good-quality versions of each for $20 or less—meters are more precise) because you can really zero in on exactly what you like. For me, our kraut is usually tart, tasty, and ready when it's 3.2 to 3.6 pH. That's my sweet spot. Wine is often in this range too. If your kraut is less than 4 pH though, it's acidified enough—meaning it's uninhabitable for most pathogenic bacteria. Kombucha is generally good to go and, I think, tastiest in the 2.5 to 3.5 pH range.

Pounders

These guys make quick work of pounding down on and packing all sorts of fermented veggies into jars, crocks, and buckets. They're also often referred to as a tamper, masher, kraut crusher, or even as "Bob" by one of Liz's friends. Her friend named it after her RIP friend Bob whose she inherited. So blow off some steam and reach for your POUNDER! Or Bob.

Smokers

Even though they have a shitty name, we love our electric Big Chief and Little Chief smokers. They're manufactured by Smokehouse Products just up the Columbia River from Portland in Hood River. They're super affordable, very simple (plug and play, no temperature settings), and durable. The Little Chiefs have a roughly 40- to 50-minute cycle, depending on what type of wood chips you use. If you want more precision, however, or if you want to cold-smoke, you should spend some more money and opt for a temperature-controlled smoker.

Vitamix or Another Strong, High-Powered Blender

If you're going to get into making our cheeses (pages 133-147), then you're going to need a high-powered blender—something like a Vitamix or a Blendtec. You can try using a cheapie for the cheeses, but I'm guessing that the hazelnut, cashew, or sunflower seed blending required will burn out the motor pretty dang quick.

The good news is, you can find plenty of refurbished models (I've used refurbished for years) on their respective company websites and beyond. That typically shaves off some bucks, though you're still looking at upward of $200 and more likely upward of $300. They're badass, though. Most are self-cleaning and crazy durable, and many double up as ice-cream makers, soup makers (they actually heat the soup!), etc.

Water Filters

See page 10.

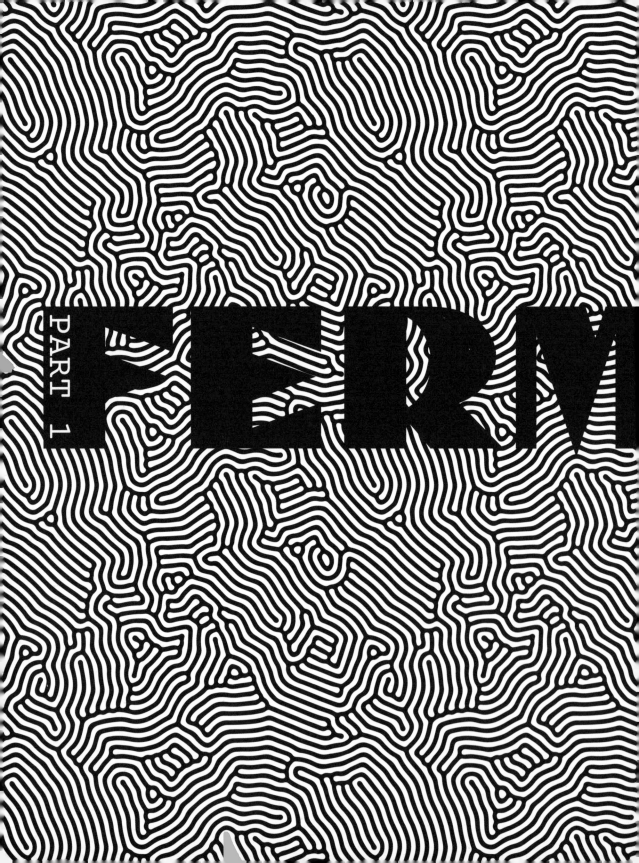

PART 1

FERM

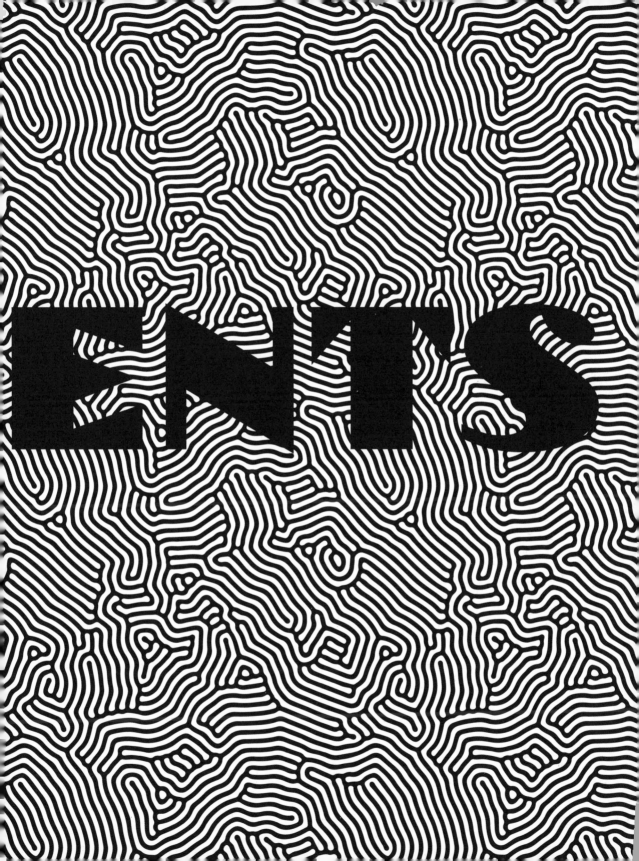

Let's Make Tasty Ferments and Learn about Stuff!

I love Mary Oliver and that very famous line from her poem "The Summer Day": "Tell me, what is it you plan to do / with your one wild and precious life?" That line in particular really stirs me. Sometimes I'm crippled by anxiety and worry I'm not honoring the spirit she was getting at with that question. But then I remember that what I want and what other people want is so incredibly varied. I'm following through on my plan for my wild and precious life: I'm a cook and I'm damn grateful to be one.

There have been times I've regretted my career, especially when I look at my bank account balance. But I have no real regrets, other than wishing I was better at what I do and that I could have a higher capacity to feed more people. That being said, I'm still immensely proud of what we make and do at Fermenter.

The foundation of what we serve at Fermenter is in the crocks and jars and fermentation vessels that line our shelves and pantry—the white and fluffy molds creeping over rice and beans, the vats of all different-colored and -flavored kombuchas and vinegars (pages 100-112). It's step 1 of flavor building for us, in terms of building acidity, savoriness, and uniquely funky flavors in all our dishes.

So think of all the food and drink ferments in this section, Part 1 of the book, in the same way. They're your new funky friends. They're super delicious on their own, and each and every one of them is a building block for, and goes into, one or more recipes in Part 2. In other words, they love one-on-one time, but they all play very well with others. Have fun!

Eat Your Salty, Sour Vegetables!

My professional introduction to fermentation was through sauerkraut. Of course I'd utilized tons of fermentation in kitchens over the years, but those ferments were all made by others: bottles of vinegar, buckets of soy sauce, tubs of miso, and barrels of sauerkraut, all bought from local purveyors. I didn't attempt to make sauerkraut on my own in the kitchen until I started working in an anarchist collective café in Portland called the Red & Black Cafe.

We bought some pretty terrible ingredients at the local Cash & Carry to piece together some not-great-food, all served super slow out of our filthy yet fun kitchen. It was a far cry from the fine dining I was used to, but I was newly vegan and super interested in the collective model. For our tempeh Reuben, we used canned sauerkraut that was dead and vinegary.

I wanted to improve things, so I started making kraut in the basement there in old 5-gallon Kikkoman buckets. It was a revelation to me. I was so excited to make this beautiful live food. The dream died, however, when another prep cook mistook the pound sign in my recipe and used 10 whole large cabbages rather than 10 pounds of cabbage. They also insufficiently salted, oh, around 40 pounds of cabbage with about three ounces of salt (way too little). It all rotted into a heaping and disgusting mess. Thereafter, I was convinced that it was probably safer for the general public for us to purchase that aforementioned canned deathbed kraut.

But fear not! It's not hard to follow the recipes in this section. Just read them through, and if you get to thinking something is off, go grab a friend and make sure you're not just being silly.

Humble Beginnings

The first ferment I remember making on my own, and not in a restaurant kitchen, was nearly 20 years ago: sour pickles from Sandor Katz's *Wild Fermentation: The Flavor, Nutrition, and Craft of Live-Culture Foods*. I picked up a copy of his book at Portland's People's Food Co-op, where I volunteered as a hands-on owner—a HOO if you want to sound like Dr. Seuss. I was volunteering in produce and there were a ton of pickling cucumbers about to go bad, so I said, "Fuck it, I'll save them. I'll ferment them!" All 20 gallons. They didn't turn out all that good flavor- and texture-wise, but they were edible. Some people loved them. Or said they did. Hippies are nice.

Part of the reason they weren't great was obvious—the cukes weren't at their prime. I also put way too much garlic in them. So there were some lessons learned.

At that time, I was kind of like, Huh, that was cool, and then I moved on to the next thing. I didn't think about fermentation much or revisit it until I started cooking at the Red & Black Café in 2008. I got a lot more into it when I opened Portobello Vegan Trattoria. There we did all sorts of fermented, plant-based cheeses. Food and drink fermentation didn't become a daily thing for me, though, until we opened Farm Spirit in 2015.

Once I'd made one or two really good ferments, I was hooked. From there on out, it was all about honing things. If I add grape leaves, then my pickles will be crispy, or if I cut the blossom ends off the cucumbers, they'll be crunchier. I used to always get kahm yeast (see What the Heck Is Kahm Yeast, Anyway?, page 11) on everything, and I couldn't figure it out. At this point I've trimmed and tightened my methods, and unless there are a whole bunch of carrots, beets, or something super sugary in my ferment, I don't get it.

I know where to put my ferments now too, how much air they need around them, and how to wash my hands and sanitize my vessels properly (see Keep It Clean, page 7). I was actually sanitizing too intensely initially. I now use a simple solution of vinegar and water in a spray bottle, and then air-dry everything. Good technique plus good sanitation is your friend when it comes to fermentation.

Sour Dills & Pickle Brine

MAKES 1 GALLON

We call our pickles "solstice pickles" because in the summer we source as many pickling cukes from nearby farms as we can, and then we enjoy the heck out of these sour dills when the days are long. Most years we empty our last buckets of them by midwinter and swear we'll make more pickles next year. To keep our dillies crisp, we use grape leaves that we pick off the fence of Buckman Elementary School's community garden, just down the street. If you can't find any grape leaves, you can also use tannin-heavy bay, oak, or even tea leaves.

I think a lot of those commercial pickling spices are way too warm-spices heavy. We wanted a house pickle that was fully sour and not too garlicky, with a clean dill taste. We push the focus instead to the fresh dill, so our sour pickles are really lively and refreshing. Also, toasting all your spices helps bring out their flavor—see page 12. Happy sour pickling!

1   Rinse the cucumbers and ever so slightly trim off their blossom ends. This helps prevent pickles from softening.

2   Place the cucumbers, garlic, grape leaves (unless you use them as a follower, step 4), fennel, coriander, peppercorns, mustard seeds, red pepper flakes, and dill in a clean nonreactive 1-gallon container. Pour the water into the vessel over the cucumbers until they are fully submerged, leaving at least 2 inches of headspace.

3   Pour about 2 cups of the water out of the vessel into another clean, easy-to-pour-from vessel. Add the salt and stir to dissolve. Pour the brine back over the cucumbers. (If I'm fermenting in a jar with a lid, I also often add the salt directly to the jar, secure the lid, and shake it until the salt dissolves.)

NOTE: Either tare/weigh your ingredients as you add them to your fermentation vessel to determine the amount of salt to add (see Tare It Up!, page 7) or simply add 6 to 7 tablespoons to taste.

****
3$^1/_2$ to 4 pounds
  small, firm pickling
  cucumbers
8 cloves garlic,
  peeled and crushed
2 fresh grape leaves
  (see Followers, page
  26)
2 teaspoons fennel
  seeds, toasted
2 teaspoons coriander
  seeds, toasted
2 teaspoons black
  peppercorns, toasted
2 teaspoons whole
  yellow mustard
  seeds, toasted
1 teaspoon red pepper
  flakes, toasted
2 stalks flowering
  dill, or 1 to 2
  bunches fresh dill
8 to 9 cups water
2 to 2.5 percent
  fine sea salt by
  weight, or 6 to 7
  tablespoons (see
  note)
****

CONTINUED

4   Top the cucumbers and brine with a follower of plastic wrap, or use the grape leaves (for more on building a ferment, see page 8). Top the follower with clean fermentation weights (see Fermentation Weights, page 26); place a lightweight, breathable cloth over the top of the vessel; and secure it with twine or a rubber band. You want the fermenting pickles to bubble and off-gas as they ferment, but you don't want any air in direct contact with them. Place the vessel in a bowl or deep dish, in case it overflows at any point during fermentation.

5   Ferment at room temperature (55 to 75 degrees F) and out of direct sunlight for 5 days and up to 2 weeks. If it's too warm, the cucumbers might get mushy and develop significant kahm yeast (see What the Heck Is Kahm Yeast, Anyway?, page 11). The colder the temperature, the slower they ferment. I usually like the flavor and crunch best in the above range because the longer the cucumbers ferment, the tarter, more pungent, and softer they get.

6   Check on them every day or so with clean or gloved hands. Keep those pickles submerged! If they're not, they might get moldy. Wipe down the inside of the fermentation vessel's headspace with a clean towel if there's any sort of buildup, then clean and rebuild your follower, weight, and cloth cover.

7   I recommend keeping a tester pickle up top to sample. As your pickles ferment, you can always add more salt to taste.

8   Every time you check on the pickles, stir the top of the brine. This helps keep the kahm yeast at bay. Once the pickles' taste and texture are to your liking, store them, submerged in the brine, in the refrigerator for up to 3 months. They keep longer than that, but become less vibrant and yummy.

NOTE: Don't discard your leftover pickle brine! Save it for backslopping future lactic ferments (page 10).

Hot Behind Hot Sauce

MAKES ABOUT 1½ CUPS

This super-simple pureed hot sauce recipe is very go-with-the-flow. Though it's great with any ripe medium-hot to hot chili, I love it the most with 100 percent–ripe red jalapeños. I also like to use fruity Jimmy Nardellos, which have way more flavor than red bells and little to no heat. Fermenter's go-to brunch hot sauce uses habaneros. Whatever chili I make it with, just about every morning I dash this fiery sauce on my brekkie scrambles. I'll even eat it straight up on toast.

If you're wondering about the name, in restaurant kitchens when you're walking behind someone you announce yourself, since everyone is moving fast in tight quarters. Typically, you say "Behind" when you aren't holding anything; "Sharp behind" when you've got a knife, cleaver, etc.; and "Hot behind" when you're carrying something just out of the oven or off the burner.

When someone says, "Hot behind," I typically reply, "Why, thank you!" because I love dad jokes. I say it over and over, to the chagrin of my coworkers. My wife tells me that the key to comedy is to wear people down with your jokes through repetition until they laugh out of desperation. When they finally offer a weak little laugh, you can heartily guffaw, victorious.

Note that two ingredients are optional: xanthan gum and vinegar. Xanthan gum thickens the hot sauce and keeps it from separating (see Xanthan Gum, page 22). If you don't use it, your sauce will be thinner but still delicious. Just give it a good shake before using it as the sauce solids will rise to the top and liquids will remain at the bottom. Vinegar adds shelf stability. It's hard to say exactly how much longer your hot sauce will last you if you add it, because of molds and conditions yada, yada, but let's say it'll give you some more weeks.

NOTE: Either tare/weigh your ingredients as you add them to your fermentation vessel to determine the amount of salt to add (see Tare It Up!, page 7) or simply add 1½ to 2 teaspoons to taste.

CONTINUED

****
½ pound fresh spicy
    chilies, stemmed and
    chopped into 1-inch
    pieces
2 cloves garlic,
    peeled
2 to 2.5 percent
    fine sea salt by
    weight, or 1½ to 2
    teaspoons (see note)
Water to cover the
    chilies (about ¾
    cup)
Pinch to ⅛ teaspoon
    xanthan gum
    (optional)
Splash to 1 tablespoon
    vinegar, for shelf
    life (optional)
****

1   Put the chilies, garlic, and salt into a clean pint jar. You'll most likely need to use a sauerkraut pounder or heavy pestle to smash the chilies down so they fit into the jar. Add water to cover, leaving about 2 inches of headspace.

2   Place a piece of plastic wrap over the top of the chilies as a follower (see Followers, page 26), then put a clean weight on top of that. Place a lightweight, breathable cloth over the top of the jar, and secure it with twine or a rubber band. You want the chilies to bubble and off-gas as they ferment, but you don't want any air in direct contact with them. Put the jar on top of a plate or bowl, in case it overflows at any point during fermentation.

3   Ferment at room temperature (55 to 75 degrees F) and out of direct sunlight for about 2 weeks. Check on the ferment every day or so, and give it a stir. This helps keep kahm yeast (see What the Heck Is Kahm Yeast, Anyway?, page 11) from taking hold (kahm yeast loves hot sauce). If there's any sort of buildup, wipe down the headspace inside the jar with a clean towel, then clean and rebuild your plastic-wrap follower, weight, and cloth cover.

4   After 2 weeks, strain the chilies and garlic, and set the brine aside. In a blender, add the chilies, garlic, and ¼ cup to ½ cup of the brine (see note), and blend on low speed for about 1 minute, or until combined but still a bit chunky. Sample it and add more brine to your liking. A ½ cup of brine is generally our sweet spot. Continue blending, moving up to the highest speed, for 3 to 4 minutes, or until the sauce is fully blended and smooth.

5   If using the xanthan gum and/or vinegar: With the blender still running, very slowly sprinkle in the xanthan gum. Don't add too much: it clumps easily. Add the vinegar. Blend for 3 to 4 more minutes.

6   Store the hot sauce in the refrigerator for up to 6 months. Shake or stir it every now and again if you don't use it often.

NOTE: Save the remaining brine for backslopping future batches (see Backslop Might Sound Gross but . . . page 10), add it to marinades or vinaigrettes, or put it in a squeeze bottle and use it as home protection. Kind of kidding.

North Coast Kraut

MAKES ABOUT 2 QUARTS

Our North Coast Kraut is crazy good.

Over the years, we've used all different varieties of bull kelp—including kombu, as well as laver/nori, wakame, dulse, sea fern, *Iridea*, and others—in this kraut. These days we use and love Naturespirit Herbs' Six Mix Seaweed Powder. Purchase it online or use any tasty, edible seaweeds you want. Make sure your seaweed is fully dry before you begin this recipe. If it's at all moist, leave it out on a baking sheet for a day or two, or dehydrate it at 150 degrees F. If your dried seaweed isn't fully ground, grind or pulse it in a coffee grinder or food processor.

A 2-quart wide-mouth glass jar works great for this recipe. If you use a plastic container, make sure it's food grade.

****
3 pounds (1 head)
   green cabbage, outer
   leaves removed
1/2 cup dried seaweed
   or seaweed blend,
   finely ground
3/4 cup (3 ounces) raw
   hulled hemp seeds
1 (1-inch) piece
   peeled fresh ginger,
   minced (about 1
   heaping tablespoon)
1 clove garlic, minced
2 to 2.5 percent fine
   sea salt by weight,
   or 2 scant to
   heaping tablespoons
   (see note)
****

1   Using a very sharp knife, place the cabbage firmly on its core and slice it in half down through the core. Quarter each half through the core and remove and discard the cores.

2   With your sharp knife or a mandoline, or using the slicing attachment on a food processor, thinly slice the cabbage (the thickness is up to you; we generally like very thin roughly 1/16-inch-thick slices). Then chop the cabbage into whatever length of pieces you want. I like bite-size 1- to 3-inchers.

3   Put the cabbage, seaweed, hemp seeds, ginger, garlic, and salt in a large bowl. Using clean or gloved hands, toss everything together. Let it sit for at least 30 minutes and up to 1 hour so that the salt can start to pull out cabbage liquid. After that, squeeze it so that it really crunches with your clean or gloved hands for 1 to 2 minutes, or until it is juicy enough that when you squeeze a handful of the cabbage over the bowl it drips.

NOTE: Either tare/weigh your ingredients as you add them to your bowl to determine the amount of salt to add (see Tare It Up!, page 7) or simply add 2 scant to heaping tablespoons to taste.

4   Tightly pack the cabbage mix into a nonreactive fermentation vessel, with at least 2 inches of headspace. You'll most likely need to use a sauerkraut pounder or heavy pestle to smash the cabbage down so it fits into the jar. Let it sit for at least 30 minutes and up to 1 hour. During this time the cabbage will continue to release water.

CONTINUED

Fermenter's #1 bestselling sauerkraut is the North Coast Kraut. People go wild over it, including my dad, who's a badass. He's always lived in the Bay Area, and scuba diving the rough waters of California's North Coast is among his favorite things. He seems more comfortable in the water than on land. He acts so much like an otter when he's diving that he got a custom-made otter wetsuit with otter ears and an otter face. So yeah, he has a soft side too.

I wanted a seaweed kraut on the Fermenter menu early on, so I developed the North Coast Kraut in my dad's otter-y honor. Though his retired homicide detective self would never admit it, he has a bit of hippie in him. He loves Janis Joplin, Iron Butterfly, and Peter, Paul, and Mary, so I threw in some hemp seeds. Got you, Dad!

5   You want the brine to now cover the cabbage when you press down on it. If it's not covering the cabbage, see page 3.

6   Top the cabbage with your preferred follower and weights (see pages 26-27). You want it to bubble and off-gas as it ferments, but you don't want any air in direct contact with it. Place the vessel in a bowl or deep dish, in case it overflows at any point.

7   Ferment at room temperature (from 55 to 75 degrees F) and out of direct sunlight for 5 days and up to 2 weeks. If it's too hot, the cabbage might get mushy, slimy, or develop significant kahm yeast (see What the Heck Is Kahm Yeast, Anyway?, page 11). The colder the temperature, the slower it ferments. I usually like the flavor and crunch best in the above range because the longer the kraut ferments, the tarter, more pungent, and softer it gets. During the fermentation process, you can add more salt to taste: just stir it into a little water before adding.

8   Check on it every day or so with clean or gloved hands. I recommend sampling the kraut each time you check on it. Always make sure the vegetables are submerged: if they aren't, they might get moldy. If there's any sort of buildup, wipe down the inside of the fermentation vessel with a clean towel. Clean and rebuild your plastic wrap follower, weight, and cloth cover.

9   Store it, submerged in the brine, in the refrigerator for up to 2 months. It keeps longer than that, but becomes less vibrant and yummy.

Pickle Kraut

MAKES ABOUT 2 QUARTS

It's just about impossible to make enough Sour Dills (page 39) to get us through the winter. Generally, no matter how many we ferment in the summer, we run out by midwinter—that's how good they are. I think the most we've ever pickled in a summer is a couple thousand pounds. That's a lot of pickles!

I was determined to come up with something to top our burger (page 163) with when we run out of our sour pickles—something with that same pickle-y, dilly crunch that we could ferment outside of summer as a stand-in. Hello, Pickle Kraut! This tasty kraut incorporates all the same pickling spices and dill as our pickles (although we use fresh dill for it rather than flowering dill), and luckily, cabbage is available year-round. FYI, we add a little pickle brine backslop to this one, so you get a bit of that OG pickle in it. It's OK to leave it out if you don't have any.

See page 12 for instructions on toasting the spices. Toast them all at the same time in one small pan.

1　Using a very sharp knife, place the cabbage firmly on its core and slice it in half down through the core. Quarter each half through the core and remove and discard the cores.

2　With your sharp knife or a mandoline, or using the slicing attachment on a food processor, thinly slice the cabbage (the thickness is up to you; we generally like very thin roughly ⅟₁₆-inch-thick slices). Then chop the cabbage into whatever length of pieces you want. I like bite-size 1- to 3-inchers.

3　Put the cabbage, dill, garlic, mustard seeds, red pepper flakes, fennel, coriander, black pepper, and salt in a large bowl. Using clean or gloved hands, toss everything together. Let it sit for at least 30 minutes and up to 1 hour. After that, crunch it with your clean or gloved hands for 1 to 2 minutes, or until it is juicy enough that when you squeeze a handful of the cabbage over the bowl it drips.

NOTE: Either tare/weigh your ingredients as you add them to your bowl to come up with the amount of salt to add (see Tare It Up!, page 7) or simply add 1½ to 2 tablespoons to taste.

4　See pages 45–46, steps 4–9, for remaining sauerkraut packing and fermenting steps. Add the optional pickle brine if you like.

```
**********************
3 pounds (1 head)
   green cabbage, outer
   leaves removed
2 bunches fresh dill,
   coarsely chopped
   (about 1¹/₂ cups)
3 cloves garlic,
   minced
2 teaspoons whole brown
   or yellow mustard
   seeds, toasted and
   coarsely ground
¹/₂ teaspoon red pepper
   flakes, toasted and
   coarsely ground
1 teaspoon fennel
   seeds, toasted and
   coarsely ground
1 teaspoon coriander
   seeds, toasted and
   coarsely ground
¹/₄ teaspoon black
   peppercorns, toasted
   and coarsely ground
2 to 2.5 percent
   fine sea salt by
   weight, or 1¹/₂ to
   2 tablespoons (see
   note)
1 cup pickle brine
   (from Sour Dills &
   Pickle Brine, page
   39; optional)
**********************
```

Lactic Acid Bacteria Know What's Best for You

A lot of people come into food and drink fermentation thinking of it as a human invention. If you conceptualize it that way, you're most likely going to set up your ferment incorrectly. You're going to think, How do I make a successful ferment? It's much better to come at it from the perspective that this whole transformation is going to happen no matter what you do. Make the conditions as hospitable to the process as possible. And then, whatever you end up with, whether it's delicious kombucha or a not-so-great mushy kraut, is not inherently a success or a failure. It's simply what was meant to be. (What a hippie idea!) Sandor Katz said something along these lines when he did a presentation at Fermenter, and it really helped me get my head wrapped around my approach.

Lactic acid bacteria is a great place to start having a really basic and foundational conversation about fermentation. It's so approachable and easy. It's much easier to start talking about lactic ferments—krauts, sour pickles, hot sauces, etc.—than about koji or tempeh, or the wide world of cheeses.

Lactic acid bacteria are literally all around us. They're on just about everything. If you understand that all food and drink ferments, lactic and otherwise, are going to happen based on the inputs, and that your job in creating a ferment is to simply create the conditions that will lead to the outcome you desire, you're on the right path.

So please don't worry about all the exact ins and outs of the recipe steps for our ferments. Instead, put time, energy, and thought into your conditions. I mean, if you carefully put together a vessel of veggies to lactic ferment, and then you put that vessel in a sunny summer window where it's blazing hot, you're most likely going to end up with a ferment with a weird slimy texture. It'll also probably have some significant off-flavors. It didn't fail, and you didn't fail—that's exactly what was meant to happen under those conditions. The conditions I want you to pay the closest attention to are temperature, humidity, and airflow.

Because human beings have lived alongside fermentation for most of time, we've refined it by creating everything from particular vessels (such as kojibans; page 27) to fermentation rooms and vacuum sealers. All that technology and equipment helps us and our ferments along. We're able to really dial things in. I aim to get

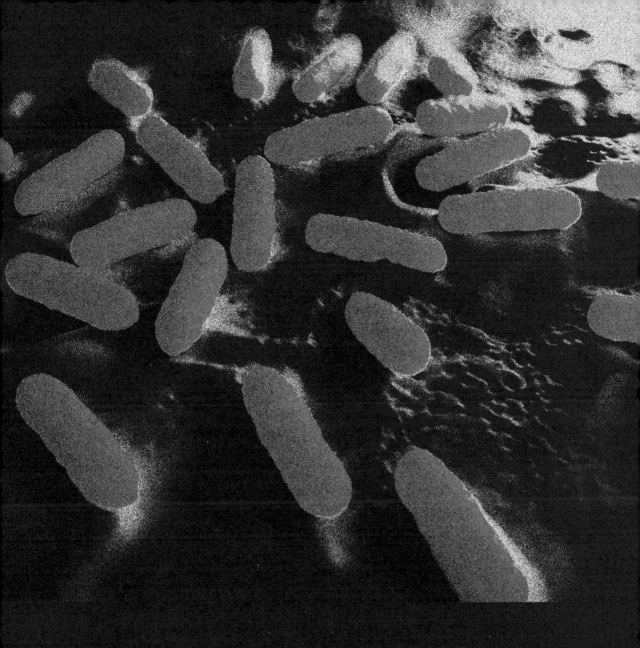

you to a place where you have a good grasp of the ideal conditions for your ferments and the know-how to hone those conditions. That's where it's at in terms of art and skill in the world of food and drink fermentation.

We all get to have this complex and super beneficial lifelong relationship with food and drink fermentation. It's so beautiful. We've cultivated this relationship as humans, and fermentation has rewarded us with so many incredibly delicious, culturally relevant foods, alongside a wealth of probiotic health. So, yeah, lactic bacteria know what's best for you. Now make them proud.

Ruby Kraut

MAKES ABOUT 2 QUARTS

I started making our Ruby Kraut because of a simple farmer mistake: we got red cabbage delivered instead of the green cabbage we'd ordered. We needed kraut, so I went ahead and used it. At first I made it with caraway, but after a while I decided to add apple and beets to it. I was worried that might be a little too much natural sugar, that the yeasts would rise to power as a result, and that it would get mushy and slimy, but it worked like a charm. It's incredible.

Although I certainly love softer and more aged krauts, I appreciate, and Fermenter makes, crunchier krauts like this one, with a nice clean acidity. We love the sweet and sour Ruby Kraut on its own and on boards, but mostly we love it on our Koji Beet Reuben (page 159).

1   Using a very sharp knife, place the cabbage firmly on its core and slice it in half down through the core. Quarter each half through the core and remove and discard the cores.

2   With your sharp knife, or a mandoline, or using the slicing attachment on a food processor, thinly slice the cabbage (the thickness is up to you; we like roughly ¹⁄₁₆-inch-thick slices). Then chop the cabbage into whatever length of pieces you want. I like bite-size 1- to 3-inchers.

3   Put the cabbage, beets, apple, garlic, horseradish, caraway seeds, and salt in a large bowl. Using clean or gloved hands, toss everything with the salt until it's fully incorporated. Let it sit for 30 minutes to 1 hour. After that, crunch the cabbage and beets (not the apple because it will crumble) with your clean or gloved hands for 1 to 2 minutes or until it is juicy enough that when you squeeze a handful of the cabbage over the bowl it drips.

NOTE: Either tare/weigh your ingredients as you add them to your bowl to determine the amount of salt to add (see Tare It Up!, page 7) or simply add 2 to 2 ½ tablespoons to taste.

4   See pages 45-46, steps 4–9, for remaining sauerkraut packing and fermenting steps.

****

3 pounds (1 medium-large head) red cabbage, outer leaves removed

³/₄ pound red beets, peeled and grated (about 3 cups)

1 sweet, tart apple, such as a Braeburn or Pink Lady, peeled, cored, and thinly sliced

1 clove garlic, minced

1-inch piece of fresh horseradish, peeled and minced (about 1 heaping tablespoon), or 2 teaspoons of high-quality prepared horseradish found in your grocer's refrigerator section

2 teaspoons caraway seeds, toasted (see Toast Your Spices, page 12)

2 to 2.5 percent fine sea salt by weight, or 2 to 2¹/₂ tablespoons (see note)

****

Spicy Giardiniera

MAKES 1 GALLON

I really wanted a classic giardiniera for Fermenter like you find on antipasti platters, but rather than pickling all the vegetables in vinegar, which is definitely the norm, I wanted to ferment ours and also make it fairly spicy. Pretty much all store-bought giardiniera is pickled with vinegar—bracingly salty and sour, with a hint of sweetness. Ours is all that, with some funk thrown in.

1   Put the cauliflower, Fresno peppers, bell pepper, carrots, celery, garlic, mustard seeds, oregano, fennel seeds, and salt in a 1-gallon jar or crock. Add the water, leaving at least 2 inches of headspace, and stir to dissolve the salt.

    NOTE: Either tare/weigh your ingredients as you add them to your jar or crock to determine the amount of salt to add (see Tare It Up!, page 7) or simply add 5 scant to heaping tablespoons to taste.

2   Top the giardiniera with your preferred follower and weights (see pages 26-27). You want it to bubble and off-gas as it ferments, but you don't want any air in direct contact with it. Place the vessel in a bowl or deep dish in case it overflows at any point.

3   Ferment at room temperature (55 to 75 degrees F) and out of direct sunlight for 5 days and up to 2 weeks. The colder the temperature, the slower the giardiniera ferments. I usually like the flavor and crunch best in the above range because the longer the giardiniera ferments, the tarter, more pungent, and softer it gets. During the fermentation process, you can add more salt to taste—just sprinkle it directly into the vessel.

4   Check on it every day or so with clean or gloved hands. I recommend sampling the giardiniera each time you check on it. Always make sure the vegetables are submerged: if they aren't, they might get moldy. If there's any sort of buildup, wipe down the inside of the fermentation vessel with a clean towel. Clean and rebuild your plastic wrap follower, weight, and cloth cover.

5   Once the giardiniera is to your liking, add the olive oil (you may need to remove some brine to do so) and stir to combine. Store it in the refrigerator for up to 2 months. It keeps longer than that, but becomes less vibrant and yummy. Be sure to give everything a good stir whenever you serve it, in order to reincorporate the olive oil.

****

2 pounds (1 head) cauliflower, trimmed and cut into small florets

4 red fresh Fresno chili peppers, or 2 to 4 medium-size, medium-hot fresh chili peppers, stemmed and thinly sliced

1 red bell pepper, diced into roughly $1/4$-inch pieces

3 to 4 medium carrots, peeled and sliced diagonally into roughly $1/8$-inch-thick slices

5 to 6 celery stalks, sliced into roughly $1/4$-inch-thick slices

5 to 6 cloves garlic, peeled and thinly sliced

1 tablespoon plus 1 teaspoon yellow mustard seeds

2 teaspoons dried oregano

1 teaspoon fennel seeds

2.5 percent fine sea salt, or 5 scant to heaping tablespoons (see note)

$2^1/_2$ quarts water

1 cup extra-virgin olive oil

****

Waste Not, Want Not

We definitely aren't at zero waste at Fermenter, but we are always striving to get closer to that. We continually look for ways to reduce food waste and single-use plastics. Last year we transformed our entire takeout program with Portland company Bold Reuse in a way that allows us to package takeaway orders in reusable, zero-waste containers. Neat!

Our walk-in refrigerator always has a good amount of containers filled with edible odds and ends—trimmings and such that we think might be tasty for a second use.

We like to get creative with our kitchen food waste. Lucky for you, fermentation is an excellent pathway for this, because it not only transforms flavor, it also often beneficially affects texture. Here are some ways we turn your kitchen scraps into deliciousness that you can easily rock at home.

SEEDS Fermented Squash Guts!

Whenever you clean any sort of squash, we recommend that you collect the guts—seeds and all—add a little salt (roughly 2 to 2.5 percent: see Tare It Up!, page 7) and water to the mix (just enough so you can stir them), and ferment them for a week or so. You can then puree and pass the guts through a sieve, or juice them and use the resulting liquid as an inexplicably awesome base for a sauce. Or after fermenting, dehydrate and then grind the seeds into a coarse powder, and add them to seasoning salts or use them to top a pie, crumble, or savory dish.

STEMS Stemmy Kraut or Kimchi!

Do you have stems from leafy greens like mustard, mizuna, spinach, arugula, etc.? Coarsely chop them and add some minced garlic and ginger; leftover pulp from strained hot sauce, if you've got it; and salt (roughly 2 to 2.5 percent: see Tare It Up!, page 7). Cover your jar or crock with all the things (see pages 8-9) and let it get yummy funky for 1 to 2 weeks, like a kraut or kimchi. If the stems are quite fibrous, maybe blend them into a dumpling or pasta filling?

SKINS Flavor Bomb for Vinegars, Booches, Kefirs & Ginger Beers!

A lot of people just don't understand how much flavor, and how many
nutrients, are in veggie and fruit skins. At Fermenter, we often
save them and throw them whole into all sorts of things—including our
vinegars, booches, kefirs, and ginger beer—for a flavor boost. And
if the skin is less fibrous and more tender—I'm thinking of tomato,
carrot, and potato skins—we often dehydrate them and then grind them
into a powder. We use those colorful, flavorful powders in various
seasoning blends, sauces, etc.

Mold Is Gold

Molds are so universally off-putting and disgusting, it's just insanely amazing to me that some hardworking-as-hell folks out there decided to straight-up domesticate them, like they were breeding dogs or cats, to make delicious and useful things for people. I mean, don't get me started on the domestication of wild *Aspergillus*.

The folks who, thousands of years ago, figured out how to coax sugars out of grains with molds so they could get drunk off rice wine are heroes of human history. And let's not forget the absolute geniuses in Indonesia who created processes for stitching molds around soybeans wrapped in banana leaves for tempeh. What the heck?! Amazing. To continue to refine and learn how to make savory pastes, delicious mold-ripened cheeses, and misos and garums with the use of molds is so absolutely astounding. Us humans should be pretty proud of our ancestors for being so brave and awesome.

Chickpea Miso

MAKES 1 QUART (ABOUT 2 POUNDS)

In Portland, we're very lucky to have local miso makers Earnest and Yuri Migaki of Jorinji Miso. They're artisans who've been at it for years, and their organic, non-GMO misos are amazing. I love their six-month white miso and their eight-month lima bean miso, as well as their three-year dark red. We use their misos when we want some finer, aged flavor in a dish; we don't have the space at Fermenter to age ours as long as they do.

We do, however, love this quick and easy one-month chickpea miso. We use it in our Miso Sauce (page 161), Boneless Broth (page 195), aged cheeses (pages 141-146), and all sorts of yummy Fermenter dishes. When you soak and then cook the chickpeas for this recipe, please don't forget to reserve the soaking/cooking water (a.k.a. aquafaba): you'll need ½ to ¾ cup to add to the miso. Or you can save it all (it keeps, refrigerated, for up to 2 weeks) to make our yummy and versatile Aquafaba Mayo (page 201). If so, simply use filtered water below instead of reserving the cooking water.

```
*********************
1 cup dried chickpeas
8 cups water
2³/₄ cups Koji Rice
  (about 1 pound)
  (page 63) or store-
  bought koji rice
5 percent fine sea salt
  by weight, or 2¹/₂ to
  3 tablespoons, plus
  about ¹/₂ teaspoon
  for salting the top
  of the miso
*********************
```

1 In a colander or fine-mesh sieve, rinse the chickpeas. Put the chickpeas in a medium bowl, cover them with the water, and soak overnight (for 12 or more hours).

2 Pour the soaked chickpeas and their soaking water into a medium pot, and bring to a boil over high heat. Lower the heat to medium and lightly boil the chickpeas, periodically skimming off and discarding any foam, for 30 to 40 minutes, or until they are tender and cooked through.

3 In a colander or fine-mesh sieve, drain the chickpeas, reserving the cooking water. Put the chickpeas in a medium bowl and mash them with a potato masher, pulse them in the bowl of a food processor, or grind them in a meat grinder to a consistency anywhere from chunky to super smooth (we lean toward a coarse mash at Fermenter). Set them aside to cool.

CONTINUED

4   When the chickpeas are cool enough to handle, using clean or gloved hands, mix in the Koji Rice, breaking up any koji clumps as you do, until it is fully incorporated. Add the reserved chickpea cooking water, 2 tablespoons at a time (if you're reserving the cooking water to make Aquafaba Mayo, then just use filtered water here), mixing it in by hand until it is the consistency of a thick chunky hummus and you can easily pack it into moist, plum-size balls that don't crumble.

NOTE: Either use our scale plus tare technique to determine the amount of salt to add (for more on this see page 7), or simply use 2½ to 3 tablespoons. Add the salt, and mix thoroughly.

5   Using clean or gloved hands, pack about 1 cup of the miso at a time into a clean quart jar. Really pack it in to eliminate air pockets, leaving about 2 inches of headspace. Smooth the top of the miso, wipe down the inside of your jar, and sprinkle the remaining ½ teaspoon of salt evenly on top of the miso. Place a piece of plastic wrap over the top of the miso—right on it—as a follower (see Followers, page 26), then put a clean weight on top of that. Place a lightweight breathable cloth over the top of the jar, and secure it with twine or a rubber band. Store it at room temperature (55 to 75 degrees F) and out of direct sunlight for 1 month and up to 6 weeks.

6   Check on the miso every few days—please taste it each time! You'll learn a lot about the transformation if you try it at different points along the way. If there's mold on top, scrape it off and discard it. If there's tamari (the bit of liquid that often pools on top of miso) on top, either stir it back into the miso or leave it to collect and spoon it off at the end to cook with. Smooth the top of the miso (don't add more salt), wipe down the inside of the jar with a clean towel if there's any sort of surface mold buildup, and clean and rebuild your plastic wrap follower, weight, and cloth cover. When the miso is to your liking, store it in the refrigerator for up to 6 months.

Koji Rice

MAKES ABOUT 2 QUARTS

Koji is the Japanese name for several varieties of molds, including the *Aspergillus oryzae* in this recipe, used for all sorts of culinary applications. The roots of koji, however, go all the way back to ancient China and shortly thereafter Japan. The history of koji mold is fascinating, and if you haven't read it already, we highly recommend our friends Jeremy Umansky and Rich Shih's book, *Koji Alchemy: Rediscovering the Magic of Mold-Based Fermentation*.

I love making koji because it makes me feel connected to this millennia-old culinary tradition. Koji is often used as a pre-ferment, and it's a great way to access sugars and proteins for continued fermentation. We've been making koji rice at Fermenter for a few years. It goes into our Chickpea Miso (page 61), our Shio Koji (page 70), the Smoked Onion Shio Koji (page 71), and we also dehydrate and grind it into seasoning salts (page 184) that flavor bomb all sorts of Fermenter things, including the jojos in our Cheesy Jojo Supreme (page 183).

It never ceases to amaze me that people from ancient times were able to figure out such an unusual and complicated culinary method. You know, taking a piece of meat and putting it on the fire, scratching your furry primal chest, and smelling those immediate good smells—that makes sense. It's not so hard to imagine. Cultivating mold, on the other hand, to then make moldy rice, to then make rice wine, or savory pastes or sauces, is so complex! Koji is an incredible win for humans. Go, Team Humans!

```
***********************
4 cups uncooked,
  organic rice (we use
  medium-grain rice
  from Polit Farms),
  rinsed
1/2 teaspoon koji
  spores (page 22),
  see note
***********************
```

1. In a colander or fine-mesh sieve, rinse the rice until the water runs clear. In a medium bowl, cover it with water by a few inches and soak overnight (for 12 or more hours).

2. Fill a steaming pot one-quarter to half full with water, allowing at least 2 inches, preferably 3 to 5 inches, between the water and your steamer, and bring to a boil.

3. Line a 12-inch bamboo steamer or stainless perforated steaming pan with muslin or cheesecloth. Evenly spread the rinsed, soaked, and drained rice in it. You want the rice to be no more than 2 inches deep.

4. Once the water is boiling, with oven mitts or a kitchen towel, carefully place the steamer on the pot, and steam the rice for about 1 hour, until slightly tender.

CONTINUED

1   Cool steamed rice on muslin or other lint-free cloth.

2   Inoculate it with koji spores.

3   Bundle it up and transfer it to the incubator.

4   After 24 hours, put koji rice in cloth-lined deep casserole dish or kojiban, and top with slightly damp towel or cloth to continue incubating.

5   Remove koji from incubator after curing 18 to 24 more hours and check out those koji rice chunks!

6   Break it all apart and enjoy.

5   At about the 30-minute mark, check the water level and toss the rice with a fork. Add more hot water if it's getting low. You want it to ultimately be the texture and bite of leftover takeout rice that you left in the fridge a bit too long.

6   With oven mitts or a kitchen towel carefully remove the rice-filled steamer from the pot.

7   Lay out a lint-free muslin cloth, and spread the steamed rice onto it. Break the rice apart with a fork. Let it cool until it is right around 90 degrees F. This should take 20 to 40 minutes. You can speed things up by fluffing the rice with a fork periodically.

8   Transfer the right-around-90-degree rice to a large bowl (hang onto the cloth or towel it was on), and use a koji spore shaker (a.k.a. a powdered sugar shaker with a piece of cheesecloth situated under the lid, page 28) to evenly dust the rice with the koji spores.

9   Using clean or gloved hands, or a fork or spoon, mix the rice with the koji spores until the spores are well incorporated.

10 Transfer the inoculated rice back to the cloth or towel, and gather the fabric at the top and knot or tie off the top.

11 Put the koji satchel into your warm, slightly humid incubator (page 80) set to 89 degrees F with a pan of water situated on the bottom.

12 Refill the pan of water if it runs dry at any point during incubation. We find that with the Brød & Taylor folding proofer (page 23) set to 89 degrees, and with the water pan filled with ¼ cup water, that it runs dry after several hours.

13 Our koji rice typically takes about 48 hours to reach full growth, but that shifts throughout the year. After 24 hours, open up your koji satchel, break the koji apart (it should be quite hot and clumpy), and then put it into a cloth-lined deep casserole dish, or directly into a cedar kojiban (page 27). If you don't break up the koji, you'll likely get a very Instagrammable big chunky white piece of it. It looks pretty cool intact, but the koji spores won't penetrate as well.

14 Make a ¼-inch or so groove in the top of the rice if you'd like. I like! That's a traditional way to do it. A spiral is nice. Groove it like a little Zen sand garden. This allows for more air penetration.

15 Top the koji with a slightly damp, not too thick and not too thin, kitchen towel or cloth—think flour-sack material. Rehydrate the towel/cloth once or twice during incubation as it dries.

CONTINUED

16 Put the koji back into the incubator set to 89 degrees F, and cure it for 18 to 24 more hours, until it has an incredible aroma and white mold growth throughout, and is pretty chunky and snowy white.

17 For most of this period, the koji will be hotter than your incubation chamber. That's good. That means that the *Aspergillus* is doing its job. You just want to keep the internal temperature of the koji below 105 degrees F (use an instant-read thermometer to check), at which point the *Aspergillus* can die off.

18 If it gets close to this temperature, simply prop open the incubator or allow for more airflow in your setup, for 15 to 20 minutes. You might even turn down the heat, or turn it off entirely, for periods throughout these 18 to 24 hours.

19 Once done, remove the koji from the incubator, and with clean or gloved hands break it apart. Set it aside to cool at room temperature for 30 to 40 minutes.

20 Enjoy and use the koji right away, tightly contain and refrigerate it for up to 2 weeks, or freeze it for up to 3 months. You can also dehydrate it at the lowest temperature of your dehydrator for several hours until it is completely dry, then tightly contain it and store it at room temperature for several months.

KOJI RICE CHEAT SHEET

What temperature should my incubation chamber be set to?
Around 89 degrees F.

What level of humidity am I aiming for in it?
Around 50 to 75 percent.

What type of rice is best for koji?
An organic medium-grain sticky rice, although you can make it with any rice.

What if my koji spore package instructions are different from yours?
All koji spores are not the same, so please cross-reference our called-for volume with the manufacturer's and adjust accordingly.

How about I huff some koji spores while I'm at it?
Don't be a dummy. When casting tempeh or koji spores, please wear face protection (we all have masks now! Hi, COVID!) so that you don't inhale the spores. They are very fine and light. You don't want to inhale them unless you want a mycelium network to take root in your lungs.

What about those cool cedar trays I've seen people use for their koji?
It wasn't until I started using cedar trays to culture it that things really clicked for me with koji making. The cedar trays (known in Japan as *kojibutas* and *morobutas*, page 27) do a really good job modulating moisture. I can culture koji in a lot of different vessels now that I've learned the ins and outs. If you're just trying your hand at koji making, I highly recommend using a cedar koji tray.

Koji Is So Hot Right Now, You Guys!

Koji is definitely having a moment in the Western world right now. Unfortunately, us Westerners have a penchant for "discovering" things that have already been around for thousands of years and running wild with those things without properly giving credit where credit is due.

Don't get me wrong, I think it's neat to see all the "new" koji-based things that chefs and makers are coming up with. I see a wide variety of new specialty products—everything from so-called modern misos, cheeses, and breads, to hot sauces—all utilizing the power of koji to layer and access new flavors and add nuance. Of course, we here at Fermenter make tons of Koji Rice (page 63) that goes into our Shio Koji (page 70), our Chickpea Miso (page 61), and makes a whole bunch of our dishes leaps and bounds better.

That being said, I think it's really darn important to understand and know the traditional applications of koji, its history, and origins. Koji is the Japanese name for a group of domesticated molds that came from China around 300 BCE. It was primarily used for making soy sauce, fermented bean pastes, and rice wine. Today it is still most widely used for the production of those foodstuffs. When I ask folks if they've heard of koji and they say no, I let them know that in all likelihood they consume a great deal of it unknowingly.

I haven't come across one person who hasn't had miso, sake, rice wine, or soy sauce. It immediately becomes more familiar to them, when I tell them that those delicious things all exist thanks to koji. That's how they make the connection. This thing—koji rice—that we serve in all different iterations is not a cool new food trend, but rather just another application of an old and amazing food technology. We should all be very, very grateful to the wise and intrepid folks who figured it all out originally.

Shio Koji

MAKES 1 QUART

****

$3^1/_4$ cup plus 1
  tablespoon Koji Rice
  (page 63) or store-
  bought koji rice
2 tablespoons fine sea
  salt
2 cups plus 2
  tablespoons water

****

We have a few customers who love nothing more than dipping their pizza straight up into our shio koji, like a vegan ranch. I get it. Someone once described shio koji to me as kind of like a natural teriyaki sauce, and although it doesn't taste anything like teriyaki to me, it does add its signature sweetness, savoriness, and viscosity to anything you add it to. Let's all just agree from here on out that shio koji is its own amazing thing, OK?

At Fermenter, we use ours for all sorts of things, including as a marinade for our tempehs (pages 77–95) and married with caramelized and smoked onions for our Almost Famous Fermenter Burger (page 163), as well as for a bunch of dressings and dipping sauces. The sweetness that shio koji brings to the table is so compelling and unique, in large part because the sweetness is thanks to enzymatic action as opposed to added sugars.

1   In a medium bowl, using clean or gloved hands, rub and crumble together the Koji Rice and salt. Transfer it to a clean quart jar or fermenting vessel, and add the water. Stir to combine. Wipe down the inside headspace of your jar, place a piece of plastic wrap directly on top of the shio koji, cover the jar in breathable cloth, and secure it with twine or a rubber band. Ferment at room temperature (55 to 75 degrees F) and out of direct sunlight for 5 to 7 days.

2   Every day, remove the cloth and follower, and stir (taste it if you want!). After 5 days, it should be nearly done. The longer it ferments, the more sour and lactic it gets.

3   In the bowl of a high-powered blender, puree the shio koji for 10 to 15 seconds, until it's fairly smooth and the consistency of a yogurt drink. Feel free to puree it for less time if you'd like it coarser. Enjoy right away, or refrigerate up to 1 month.

NOTE: You can also strain the shio koji rather than puree it, and use the liquid to culture things, or add it to marinades and vinaigrettes. To strain, use a cheesecloth-lined sieve over a bowl or pan, and weigh down the shio koji. Keep the reserved koji rice! We dehydrate and grind ours into an enzymatic powder for things like our Koji Seasoning Salt (page 184), koji pickles, tempura batter, kimchi, or anything that can use a little of that awesome koji flavor.

Smoked Onion Shio Koji

MAKES ABOUT 1 QUART

Our Almost Famous Fermenter Burger's (page 163) secret weapon is this Smoked Onion Shio Koji.

   With this recipe you've got enough for a whopping 20 Fermenter burgers. If you don't see yourself making that many, it also moonlights as a really tasty dipping sauce with all that smoky savory flavor. Or spoon some into your barbecue sauce (or ours! page 171), and thank me later. I also recommend marinating mushrooms with it before grilling or broiling them, and anything else you want to add savory umami to. Grilled tomato wedges love it, btw.

1   In a large, heavy-bottomed pot over high heat, combine ¾ cup of the water, the sunflower oil, and salt, then cover with a lid and bring to boil.

2   Once boiling, add the onions, stir to combine, and return the lid.

3   Cook covered for about 20 minutes, stirring every few minutes, until most of the water has evaporated and the onions start to sizzle.

4   Remove the lid, stir the onions, and reduce the heat to medium-low. In a small bowl, add the remaining 1 tablespoon of water and stir in the baking soda. Add this baking soda slurry to the onions, and stir to incorporate.

5   Cook the onions for an additional 40 to 50 minutes, stirring every couple of minutes, until they are caramelized and golden brown.

6   Remove from heat, stir in the liquid smoke, and cool to room temperature. Transfer the onions to a blender or food processor. Puree for 1 to 2 minutes, until they are the consistency of applesauce. Add the Shio Koji and puree for 2 to 3 minutes, until it is the consistency of gravy.

7   Use immediately, refrigerate for up to 2 weeks (give it a stir every few days as it continues to culture in the fridge—expanding and separating), or freeze for up to 3 months.

NOTE: We smoke this marinade at Fermenter in shallow dishes for about 1 hour, but I realize that for such a small amount you might not want to. However, if you have other things to smoke in the book— Tempeh Bacon or Smoked Pinto Bratwurst—then I recommend skipping the liquid smoke and adding this to the smoking jamboree.

```
**********************
3/4 cup plus 1
   tablespoon water,
   divided
3 tablespoons
   sunflower oil, or
   other neutral oil
1 teaspoon kosher salt
3 1/2 pounds yellow
   onions, thinly
   sliced
1/4 teaspoon baking
   soda
1/4 to 1/2 teaspoon
   liquid smoke (see
   note)
2 cups Shio Koji (page
   70) or store-bought
   shio koji
**********************
```

Koji Beets

MAKES ABOUT 4 POUNDS

Our comrades-in-koji chef Jeremy Umansky of Larder and friend Rich Shih shared this method for koji vegetable charcuterie in their excellent book *Koji Alchemy*. We've changed it ever so slightly based on our own interpretations and uses, which is exactly what Rich taught us all to do when I took his koji workshop several years ago.

You'll end up with nearly 2 pounds more of the koji beets here than you will need for our Koji Beet Reuben (page 159), because they are so dang good. And they take the better part of a week to make, so go big! These beets have years of deep and smoky sweet flavor. *Beets* the pants off bacon for us vegans. Use the extras in salads, on snack boards, in braises and stews, or refrigerate or freeze them for future sandwiches.

There's a little bit of a learning curve when it comes to the Koji Beets, but once you've got it, you've got it forever. Feel free to try this koji technique on other vegetables too. Play around!

For the best results, you've got to smoke your beets, so get out both your dehydrator and your smoker for this one. There's no way around it. Maybe fill up all the smoker racks with all sorts of tasty treats and make it a Tempeh Bacon (page 88), Smoked Onion Shio Koji (page 71), Coffee BBQ Sauce (page 171), Smoked Pinto Bratwurst (176), and Koji Beets kinda weekend?!

> **NOTE:** What you want to stay away from here are huge overgrown beets. They have a tendency to be kind of flavorless. Go for the medium ones.

BOIL & PEEL TAKES: ABOUT 2 HOURS

In two large pots, add the beets, cover them with a few inches of water, and bring to a boil.

Boil for 45 minutes to 1 hour, or until the beets are tender when pierced with a knife.

Drain the beets in a colander, and then cover them with a clean towel so that they cool slowly.

CONTINUED

```
**********************
7 pounds (about 10
  to 12 medium) red
  beets, stems trimmed
  to 1/2 inch and
  scrubbed, see note
Applewood or another
  fruit wood, for
  smoking
3 tablespoons fine sea
  salt
1 1/2 to 1 3/4 teaspoons
  koji spores (page
  22)
**********************
```

Once cool enough to handle, after 30 to 40 minutes, peel the beets by hand or with the aid of a paring knife, and remove the stem ends and discard. If any of your beets are really large, the size of a grapefruit let's say, halve them.

SMOKE & SALT TAKES: ABOUT 2 DAYS

Prepare your smoker. If it has a temperature gauge, set it to the lowest temperature possible.

Once the smoker is smoking, put the beets in it with a pan of ice water on the bottom right above your heat source, so that the beets don't dry out. Smoke them for about 1 hour over apple wood or another fruitwood.

Remove the beets from the smoker and transfer them to a large bowl. Add the salt and toss to evenly cover the beets with it.

Tightly contain and refrigerate the beets for 48 hours. (If you don't tightly contain them, your entire refrigerator will smell like a smokehouse. Trust me.)

INOCULATE TAKES: 34 TO 38 HOURS

Remove the beets from the refrigerator, gently pat them dry, and transfer them to a wire rack on top of a rimmed baking sheet. Organize the beets in rows, making sure that none are touching.

Use a koji spore shaker (a.k.a. a powdered sugar shaker with a piece of cheesecloth under the lid, page 28) to lightly and evenly dust the beets with the koji spores. Flip the beets and fully and evenly dust the other side.

Transfer the inoculated beets to your warm, slightly humid incubator (page 80) set to 89 degrees F with a small pan of water. Refill the pan of water if it runs dry at any point during incubation. We find that the Brød & Taylor folding proofer under these circumstances runs dry after several hours.

These koji beets typically take 34 to 38 hours to reach full growth, but that shifts throughout the year. Once they are completely covered in bloomy white mold, remove them from the incubator.

NOTE: When casting tempeh or koji spores, please wear face protection (we all have masks now! Hi, COVID!) so that you don't inhale the spores. They are very fine and light. You don't want to inhale them unless you want a mycelium network to take root in your lungs.

CONTINUED

1   Peel your cooled boiled beets.

2   Smoke them.

3   Salt and then refrigerate them.

4   Pat dry and then inoculate.

5   Incubate and then dehydrate them.

6   Look at your *Aspergillus*-covered
    beauties!

DEHYDRATE TAKES: 8 TO 10 HOURS
Set a dehydrator to 95 degrees F, or to your dehydrator's lowest setting.

Dehydrate the beets for 8 to 10 hours, until they are slightly shriveled and have a chewier, almost meaty texture—tender and chewy—similar to bresaola (how the heck did a cured meat make it into this cookbook?! It's just a comparison, carry on). Once they are done dehydrating, they should be roughly half the original weight of the raw and unpeeled beets that you started with.

Once dried and cooled, proceed with the Koji Beet Reuben recipe or refrigerate in a tightly lidded container, with a towel folded inside to sop up any moisture, for up to 2 weeks. You can also individually wrap them in plastic wrap, then place them in a freezer bag and freeze them for up to 3 months.

NOTE: If you have a good dehydrator with a fan, you won't need to check on the beets or rotate them or the trays as they dry. If you have a less dependable dehydrator without a fan, rotate the beets and/or the trays every couple hours so that they are evenly dehydrated.

HOW IS TEMPEH MADE?

Tempeh is made by acidifying, cooking, draining, inoculating, and incubating a substrate of legumes and/or grains. The goal is to create a firm cake of mold that knits itself in between the legumes and grains.

Acidifying

Legumes are traditionally acidified for tempeh, a necessary part of the process, by fermenting them. Dried legumes are washed, then hot-soaked and left to sour. During the process, the funky, acidified legumes get covered in a biofilm (think slime). The legumes are then washed and cooked.

We use a different approach when producing our tempeh: we acidify our substrate with vinegar. Vinegar can be added during the soaking process, while cooking the legumes or grains, or after cooking. Each renders a slightly different outcome and flavor. We prefer to acidify our legumes and/or grains by adding apple cider vinegar to the pot while we boil them.

Cooking

Legumes and grains need to be cooked for tempeh in order to set the starches and make the carbohydrates available to the molds so that they can consume them and grow. If the substrate is undercooked, the mold will not grow. If it is overcooked, however, the mold might be stunted and bogged down by too much water or too little space between the grains and beans to grow. If the mold does rise above the challenges of overcooked beans and grains and still grows, the tempeh might be too soft and mushy to actually enjoy. Bummer.

When using multiple grains and legumes, please cook them separately so that each is cooked to that "just right" state, and combine them after draining and drying.

Draining & Drying

It's important before inoculating your substrate (a.k.a. adding tempeh spores to your legumes and grains) that everything be well drained and fairly dry. Ultimately, you want a mostly dry substrate that is still warm but not hot. If it cools down significantly below the ideal incubating temperature (89 degrees F is our sweet spot), you might add several more hours to your tempeh-making process.

We use a centrifugal spinner to dry our cooked beans, but you can simply drain them and then lay them out on lint-free towels. We've

CONTINUED

1

2

3

4

1   Sort beans/legumes.

2   Cool and dry your boiled beans/legumes/grains.

3   Inoculate them with the tempeh spores.

4   Perforate your 6-inch sandwich bags.

5

6

7

8

5   Fill sandwich bags with inoculated beans/legumes/
     grains.

6   Incubate your rad tempeh.

7   Remove finished tempeh from incubator.

8   Look at your beautiful tempeh!

used blow-dryers and fans set to low and other methods to ensure our substrate isn't too wet.

Just make sure you don't overheat or dry out the substrate too much with a blow-dryer or dehydrator. Too dry or overheated cooked grains or legumes make it difficult for those rad *Rhizopus* molds to thrive.

Inoculating

We like to introduce our tempeh starter spores when the legumes and grains are dry to the touch and below 110 degrees F, but more than 80 degrees F. Again, for us, 89 degrees F is perfect. We transfer the legumes and grains to a large bowl and cast the spores over them. Be careful and thorough when mixing (maybe wear one of your trusty COVID masks that you have laying around?) so that the spores are spread evenly throughout the substrate rather than your kitchen and lungs.

For most tempeh spores, you'll want to use 2 grams of spores per 1 kilogram of cooked grains/legumes.

We say *most* because starters vary in concentration. Refer to the package's instructions—if you're lucky enough to have instructions.

Forming Cakes

These days, tempeh is commonly made and formed in perforated plastic bags. We've never seen pre-perforated bags available for it, and most small-time makers continue to perforate their bags by hand. We've had success doing so with ice picks, cake testers, and paring knives. Basically, when you make tempeh, you start with loose beans, legumes, and sometimes grains, so you need something to contain them (hello, zip-top plastic bags) so that the mold can take hold.

Traditionally, tempeh was made in banana leaves, though even in Indonesia most producers now use plastic.

Incubating

Incubating tempeh is all about trying to replicate a warm jungle environment. We shoot for fairly high humidity and a temperature right around 89 degrees F. Too cold and the mold growth might be stunted; too hot and the mold can overheat and "spore out," that is, divide into many small spores (see Sporing Out!, page 95).

Tempeh also needs different conditions during different stages of incubation. The lines are fuzzy, but in general, for the first 12 hours, go for warmth and humidity. For the last 12 hours, focus more on decent airflow and keeping the incubation chamber from getting too hot.

But where do you incubate tempeh at home? Here are some potential setups:

1   A Styrofoam cooler with a pan of water at the bottom and a thermostat controller connected to a light bulb.

2   An oven with the oven light on and a pan of water.

3   Any sort of box with a pan of water in it, placed in a warm spot in your kitchen.

4   A Brød & Taylor folding proofer (page 23) or another proofer.

5   A speed rack or other kitchen rack with a rack cover, with a humidifier or pan of water, heater, and thermostat controller.

Cooling & Storing

We prefer to make tempeh often and eat it fresh, but you can certainly also make larger batches and freeze it. Tempeh freezes remarkably well

and stores for months. If you refrigerate it, we recommend eating your tempeh within one week. Smell and appearance, as always, are the best indicators of freshness.

If you're not cooking your tempeh right away, cool it on a rack for 1 to 2 hours at room temperature, or if you kitchen is more than 80 degrees F, in the refrigerator. If you are working with slabs, carefully remove them from the plastic bags. If you are working with patties, carefully remove them from the ring molds. Refrigerate them in a lidded container, with a towel folded up inside alongside the slabs or patties to sop up any moisture and with the lid slightly askew for the first 24 hours. The following day, wipe off the condensation that accumulates, tightly lid, and refrigerate for up to 1 week, or tightly wrap the slabs or patties individually in plastic wrap, then place in a freezer bag and freeze for up to 3 months.

If you refrigerate your tempeh, do not stack it or allow it to touch other tempeh slabs or patties because the *Rhizopus* will often continue to grow and knit together even when refrigerated. Your tempeh might become a knitted-together tower of tempeh. Also, whatever you do, make sure that the tempeh has fully cooled before you pack it up. We've seen tempeh reactivate and be hot and steamy in the fridge the next day. Cultures are crazy!

Tempeh Cheat Sheet

WHAT ARE SOME GOOD LOCAL BEAN & GRAIN COMBOS?
Although we give you two distinct tempeh recipes here—one for slabs of our Pinto Bean Tempeh (page 85) as well as our Tempeh Burger Patties (page 91), which call for black lentils and millet, please know that you can make all sorts of other bean, legume, and grain combinations for either based on what you have on hand and want to use.

Here is a general guide for mixing and matching:

For our tempeh slabs: Instead of 100 percent pintos soak, cook, and use roughly 2¼ cups of any dried lentils or 2½ cups of another dried bean. If you would like to make grain + lentils or beans combo slabs I recommend 1½ cups of dried lentils, or 1¾ to 2 cups dried organic beans (1¾ cups for smaller dried beans, 2 cups for larger dried beans)—cooked the same way—combined with ½ cup to ¾ cup dried organic grains (we love millet, rice, and quinoa).

Simply rinse, soak, cook, and cool your grains as instructed in the Tempeh Burger Patties recipe—using the same amounts of vinegar and water. Then proceed with the recipe by combining the cooked grains with your beans or lentils and then inoculating. The bags will usually be bulkier if you are using 100 percent large beans, and slimmer if you are using lentils, smaller beans, or a bean or lentil plus grain mix.

For our tempeh patties: You can also sub the 2 cups dried black lentils here for small or large dried beans. You'll want 2¼ cups smaller beans and 2½ cups larger beans. Increase the cook time (same amounts of water and vinegar) to 30 to 45 minutes, until the same doneness as the lentils. You can use a different type of grain as well. Simply use the same volume and prepare as you do the millet.

WHAT IS THE WEIGHT RATIO OF HOW MUCH TEMPEH STARTER (A.K.A. TEMPEH SPORES) TO ADD TO MY SUBSTRATE?
Cooked legumes/grains: tempeh starter // 1 kilogram: 2 grams.

WHAT TEMPERATURE SHOULD MY INCUBATION CHAMBER BE SET TO?
Around 89 degrees F.

WHAT LEVEL OF HUMIDITY AM I AIMING FOR IN IT?
Around 50 to 75 percent.

WHAT CONDITIONS ARE NEEDED IN THE FIRST STAGE OF TEMPEH INCUBATION (ROUGHLY THE FIRST 12 HOURS)?
Warmth and humidity are most important.

WHAT CONDITIONS ARE NEEDED IN THE SECOND STAGE OF TEMPEH INCUBATION (ROUGHLY THE LAST 12 HOURS)?
Once the tempeh is producing its own heat, keep things from getting too hot and promote ample airflow.

Pinto Bean Tempeh

MAKES 2 (1-POUND) SLABS

****

$2^1/_2$ cups organic pinto
  beans
4 quarts cooking water
$^1/_4$ cup Apple Cider
  Vinegar (page 100)
$^3/_4$ teaspoon tempeh
  spores (page 22)

****

When you purchase store-bought tempeh in the United States, for the most part you get dry, compressed, monocropped, mass-produced soy tempeh. I love tempeh that is not that. I love local tempeh—tempeh that celebrates local beans, legumes, and grains. Our tempehs are not a meat substitute: they are their own super-delicious thing. What I look for in tempeh is a nice moist texture, as well as a flavor all its own. Tempeh should never, ever be just a foil for other flavors—there is so much nuance to it.

Be patient when making tempeh. There is definitely a learning curve. It's one of the most temperamental ferments I make. If you've never made it before, I highly recommend flipping back to page 3 before you do and reading my advice on incremental change and controls in terms of fermentation, and also reading about various local bean and grain combos (page 82) in our Tempeh Cheat Sheet.

For this recipe, get out your gloves, mask, incubator, and maybe even a blow-dryer. When working with spores especially, but really any ferments, make sure you have really clean hands (get out that fingernail brush!), or slap on some gloves. The gist: Don't expect to be a wiz from the start. Do the work and make small changes here and there. Before you know it, you'll be fermenting delicious tempeh at home.

SORT, CLEAN & SOAK TAKES: 12 OR MORE HOURS
Lay out your beans on a baking sheet or large platter, then sort out any pebbles, dirt clods, random grains, or any other undesirables and discard them. Give them a good rinse in a colander.

Put the beans in a large bowl and cover them with water by a few inches. Soak them overnight (12 or more hours).

BOIL & DRY TAKES: 30 MINUTES TO 1 HOUR-PLUS
In a large pot, bring the water and Apple Cider Vinegar to a boil.

Prepare a baking sheet by laying muslin or a lightweight, lint-free, clean towel on it. Drain the soaked beans and add them to the pot. Fully boil the beans for 30 to 45 minutes, until they are a bit undercooked but still easy to squish between your ring finger and your thumb. (Use your ring finger because it's generally a bit weaker than your index finger. I learned this trick from Portland tempeh maker Jon Westdahl of Squirrel & Crow Soy-Free Tempeh.)

CONTINUED

Drain the cooked beans in a colander, then transfer them to the baking sheet. Air-dry at room temperature for 10 to 25 minutes.

Cool the beans down until an instant-read thermometer registers between 90 and 100 degrees F before you add the tempeh spores.

> **NOTE:** You don't want the beans to get much cooler than 90 degrees, because you would then need to warm them back up to that sweet spot of 89 degrees F through and through that you are aiming for during incubation. If they cool too quickly, go ahead and cover them with a towel to keep them warm. Dramatically cooling them down and then heating them back up can add hours to your overall tempeh-making time.

You can speed things up by using a blow-dryer to dry the beans. Just be sure to set it to low so you don't scorch them or blow them off the sheet. You want everything to lose its shine (at first the beans and legumes will be wet and shiny) and become fairly dry. You don't want much water on the surface of the beans.

INOCULATE & FORM TAKES: 10 TO 15 MINUTES
Using clean or gloved hands, transfer the beans to a large, clean bowl. Carefully add the tempeh spores (be sure to wear one of your trusty COVID masks that you have laying around), and mix them in by hand until they are well incorporated.

Use an ice pick, toothpick, the end of a paring knife, or a cake tester to poke tiny holes in two (6-inch-wide zip-top) plastic bags in a ½-inch grid throughout.

Divide the inoculated pintos evenly between the two bags (about 3 to 3¼ cups per bag), making sure to get them into the corners of the bags. Pack the bags fairly tight so that there are no divots or creases. Undesirable growth often occurs in these spots if you don't fill them in.

INCUBATE TAKES: 24 TO 48 HOURS
Transfer the tempeh to your incubator (page 80) set to between 80 and 90 degrees F (89 degrees F is our sweet spot) with a small pan of water for humidity. Refill the pan with water if it dries out at any point.

> **NOTE:** Incubating tempeh is all about trying to replicate a warm jungle environment. You can use your oven with the pilot light or interior light turned on, a cooler with a hot water bottle or small heating pad, a mini greenhouse, etc. DIY it, baby (page 80)! You just want a decent amount of airflow and humidity right around 75 percent. Too cold and the mold growth might be stunted. Too hot and the mold can overheat, perish, or spore out.

Our tempeh typically takes about 24 hours to reach full growth, but that shifts throughout the year. You don't need to flip or rotate the tempeh as the mold develops, but if you are making a large batch—double what this recipe calls for, or more—I recommend moving the bags around in your incubator once or twice. Move them from top to bottom, or side to side.

> **NOTE:** You can as much as quadruple this recipe if you are using the Brød & Taylor folding proofer (page 23) and you have the extra rack for it. Put four bags of tempeh on the top rack and four bags on the bottom rack.

After 12 hours, begin checking the temperature of the tempeh simply by placing your hands on it. Once the tempeh begins to emit its own heat and feels warm to the touch, reduce the heat or turn it off entirely. You can also prop open your incubator. You don't want the tempeh to overheat. The ideal interior temperature range for it is between 85 and 95 degrees F. If you have one, carefully insert an instant-read thermometer to check its temperature now and again.

After 12 to 18 hours, the spores should be apparent. When the tempeh is done, anywhere from 24 to 48 hours, the slabs will be a solid and snowy white throughout, and fairly firm. If you're not using your tempeh right away, see page 80 for how to store it.

Tempeh Bacon

****
2 packed cups brown
  sugar
1¼ teaspoon kosher
  salt
¼ teaspoon smoked
  paprika
1 tablespoon blackstrap
  molasses
1 batch of Pinto Bean
  Tempeh (page 85),
  or 2 pounds store-
  bought tempeh
¼ cup sunflower oil,
  or other neutral oil
Applewood or another
  fruitwood, for
  smoking

****

MAKES 2 (1-POUND) SLABS

For our first attempts at tempeh bacon at Fermenter, we went barefoot down the super-duper hippie path of a cure of soy sauce, liquid smoke, oil, etc. I hated it. We tried so many approaches like that until I said, "We're overthinking this—let's make our tempeh bacon the way that real-ass pork bacon is made."

From that day forward, we've used a mix of dark brown sugar, salt, and other seasonings to cure our tempeh bacon, and then we brush it all off and smoke it. One thing obviously missing is fat. So we add oil! It's decidedly not bacon, and I love it. It hits those bacony notes that vegans often miss and crave. I love it on our BLET (page 157), in our Hidden Willamette Valley Ranch Salad (page 197), and with all sorts of breakfast things.

You can use this bacon recipe for any tempeh, ours or store-bought. That said, I'm sorry, but you've gotta pull out the smoker for this. Liquid smoke won't cut it. Do a big batch, though, and make your next-door neighbors happy that there isn't an encroaching forest fire and gift them some.

Brush off as much of the cure as you can before smoking; otherwise your bacon will be too sweet. And don't forget to fill a pan of water over your heat source when smoking. If you don't, the bacon will be dry.

1   In a medium bowl, combine the brown sugar, salt, paprika, and molasses, and stir to combine. The molasses will clump up and that's OK. Break it up with your spoon as much as you can. This is a very dry, gritty cure.

2   In a shallow pan or dish, just large enough to fit the Pinto Bean Tempeh and bacon cure, add some of the cure, transfer the slabs to the pan or dish, and carefully turn them around in it. Add the remaining cure and make sure that all parts of both slabs are covered and packed in it. Cover and refrigerate overnight (12 or more hours).

3   Prepare your smoker. If it has a temperature gauge, set it to the lowest temperature possible.

4 Using your hands or a rubber spatula, wipe off as much of the cure as possible (see note), and place the tempeh bacon in your preheated smoker with a pan of water set underneath it on the bottom. You don't want to cook the bacon at all at this stage, just smoke it. Smoke it for 1 to 1 ½ hours with apple wood or another fruitwood.

5 Remove the bacon slabs from the smoker and cool to room temperature.

6 Place the tempeh bacon in a 1-gallon plastic zip-top bag with the sunflower oil. Move the bacon around in it so that it becomes fully coated. Remove as much air as possible from the bag, then seal it. If you have a vacuum sealer, use it. Set aside to cure at room temperature for about 2 hours.

7 Slice or dice your super-tasty tempeh bacon and sizzle it up! (See step 5 on page 157.)

8 Tightly cover and refrigerate it up to 2 weeks, or freeze for up to 3 months.

NOTE: You can reuse this tempeh bacon cure a couple times. Just cover and refrigerate it for up to 1 month. Make more bacon with it, or cure veggies or tofu in it. If you cure veggies, do so raw, then smoke and cook them.

What the Heck Is Tempeh?

Tempeh is a traditional cultured food from Indonesia, usually made with yellow soybeans and sometimes black soybeans. There are so many styles, shapes, and methods for making tempeh, but most is made with a substrate of legumes and/or grains that have been acidified, cooked, and then incubated with mold spores.

The mold spores used to knit together and blanket tempeh are most commonly *Rhizopus oligosporus* and *Rhizopus oryzae*. Traditionally, they were introduced to the tempeh by adding older tempeh to the mix, but the usual method these days is to cast pure spores suspended in a rice flour medium.

While soybeans are most commonly used for tempeh, multigrain tempehs and other bean tempehs have become increasingly common. At Fermenter, we strive to use primarily local legumes and grains for our tempeh. Since local soybeans aren't readily available, we generally stick with other legumes that are, such as lentils, black beans, and pinto beans.

Tempeh Burger Patties

MAKES 10 (¼-POUND) BURGERS (ABOUT 3 POUNDS)

By volume, our burger patties are nearly two-part uncooked black lentils, one-part uncooked millet, and all parts delicious. They get sweet and smoky from the Smoked Onion Shio Koji marinade (if you're making our burger, page 163) and after pan-frying they have a perfectly seared, moist and chewy bite. We use Raprima brand tempeh spores. That said, use whatever spores you like or can get your hands on. Tempeh is an Indonesian ferment, so we like to use Indonesian spores.

As with all tempeh recipes, you'll need superclean or gloved hands, a mask, and a proofer, or other DIY incubator, on hand before starting. If you want to dig deeper into tempeh, check out our Pinto Bean Tempeh (page 85). And if you want to experiment with other bean, legume, and grain combos, see the Tempeh Cheat Sheet on page 82. We also highly recommend Kirsten and Christopher Shockey's cookbook *Miso, Tempeh, Natto & Other Tasty Ferments* for a proper tempeh education.

> **NOTE:** We use 4-inch egg ring molds at Fermenter for our tempeh burger patties (I just remove the handles with my grinder), but you can use any ring molds, biscuit cutters, or cookie cutters. I just recommend they be as close to 4 inches in diameter and ¾ to 1 inch tall as possible.

```
***********************
2 cups dried black
   lentils
3/4 cup millet
5 quarts water,
   divided
1/4 cup plus 1
   tablespoon Apple
   Cider Vinegar (page
   100), divided
1 teaspoon tempeh
   spores (page 216)
Sunflower oil for
   pan-frying, about
   1/2 cup, or other
   neutral oil
***********************
```

SORT, CLEAN & SOAK TAKES: 12 OR MORE HOURS
Lay out your lentils on a baking sheet or large platter, then sort out any pebbles, dirt clods, random grains, or any other undesirables and discard them. Give your lentils a good rinse.

Cover them with water by a few inches in a medium bowl and soak overnight (12 or more hours).

Give your grains a good rinse. Cover them with water by a few inches in a medium bowl and soak for about 30 minutes.

BOIL & DRY TAKES: 30 MINUTES TO 1 HOUR-PLUS
In a medium pot, bring 4 quarts of the water and ¼ cup of the Apple Cider Vinegar to a boil. Drain the soaked lentils and add them to the pot. Lightly boil the lentils for 4 to 8 minutes, until they are a bit undercooked, but still easy to squish between your ring finger and your thumb. (Use your ring finger because it's generally a bit weaker than your index finger.)

CONTINUED

In a medium pot, bring the remaining quart of water and 1 tablespoon of vinegar to a boil. Once boiling, drain the soaked millet, and add it to the pot. Lightly boil it for 8 to 15 minutes, until it is tender but not mushy.

Prepare two baking sheets by laying muslin or lightweight, lint-free, clean towels on each.

Drain the cooked lentils in a colander, then transfer them to one of the baking sheets. Drain the cooked millet in a fine-mesh sieve and transfer it to the other baking sheet. Air-dry both at room temperature for 10 to 25 minutes. Fluff the millet with a fork.

Cool the lentils and millet down until an instant-read thermometer registers between 90 and 100 degrees F before you add the tempeh spores.

NOTE: You don't want the lentils or millet to get much cooler than 90 degrees, because you would then need to warm them back up to that sweet spot of 89 degrees F through and through that you are aiming for during incubation. If they cool too quickly, go ahead and cover them with a towel to keep them warm. Dramatically cooling them down and then heating them back up can add hours to your overall tempeh-making time.

You can speed things up here by using a blowdryer to dry the lentils and millet. Just be sure to set it to low so that you don't scorch them or blow them off the sheet. You want everything to lose its shine (at first the beans and legumes will be wet and shiny) and become fairly dry. You don't want much water on the surface of the beans and grains.

INOCULATE & FORM TAKES: 10 TO 15 MINUTES
Using clean or gloved hands, transfer the lentils and millet to a large, clean bowl. Carefully add the tempeh spores (be sure to wear one of your trusty COVID masks that you have laying around), and mix them in by hand until they are well incorporated.

Take a clean baking sheet, or two small baking sheets, top it with parchment paper, and lay out your 10 ring molds—silicone or metal ring molds both work great.

NOTE: If you are using the Brød & Taylor folding proofer (page 23), two quarter sheets fit perfectly with five ring molds on each. Place one of the sheets on the bottom rack of the proofer, and the other on an additional top rack. Rotate the sheets once or twice during incubation.

CONTINUED

1

2

3

4

1   Form patties in ring molds and lightly pat.

2   Cover them tightly with plastic wrap and poke
     tiny holes in it.

3   Incubate the patties.

4   Remove patties from ring molds and cool for 1 to
     2 hours.

Fill each of the rings with the lentil-millet mixture. Lightly pat the burgers on the top so that they are fairly smooth, but do not push down. You want some air gaps in the patties so that the mycelium, a.k.a. the network of tempeh spores, can easily grow throughout.

Cover the baking sheet tightly with plastic wrap. Painter's tape works well to secure the plastic wrap to the sheet/s if need be. Use an ice pick, toothpick, the end of a paring knife, or a cake tester to poke tiny holes in the plastic wrap across the top of the patties in a ½-inch grid.

INCUBATE TAKES: 24 TO 48 HOURS

Transfer the tempeh patties to your incubator set between 80 and 90 degrees F (89 degrees F is our sweet spot) with a small pan of water for humidity. Refill the pan with water if it dries out at any point.

> **NOTE:** Incubating tempeh is all about trying to replicate a warm jungle environment. You can use your oven with the pilot light turned on, a cooler with a hot water bottle or small heating pad, a mini greenhouse, etc. DIY it, baby (page 80)! You just want to have a decent amount of airflow and humidity right around 75 percent. Too cold and the mold growth might be stunted. Too hot and the mold can overheat, perish, or spore out.

Our patties typically take about 24 hours to reach full growth, but that shifts throughout the year. You don't need to flip them or rotate the pans as the mold develops. You just want to get them to a nice snowy white and then they're done.

After 12 hours, begin checking the temperature of the patties simply by placing your hands on them. Once they begin to emit their own heat and feel warm to the touch, reduce the heat or turn it off entirely. You can also prop open your incubator, oven, or cooler. You don't want the patties to overheat. The ideal interior temperature range for them is between 85 and 95 degrees F. If you have one, carefully insert an instant-read thermometer into a patty to check its temperature now and again.

After 12 to 18 hours, the spores should become apparent. When the tempeh is done, anywhere from 24 to 48 hours, the patties will be a solid and snowy white throughout, and fairly firm.

COOLING & STORING

If not cooking the tempeh patties right away, see Cooling & Storing on page 80 for how to store it.

Problems with Tempeh

SPORING OUT!

Sporulation, which looks like gray or black patches among
the white fuzzy spores, is pretty common when you're
making tempeh. A fungal colony sporulates when it becomes
stressed. Stress usually indicates some sort of impending
doom for the colony. The molds get the dire memo and want
to start propagating right away. For example, if your
incubation chamber gets too hot or too moist, or if there
isn't a good supply of food for the molds, the colony
will most likely sporulate. It's their valiant attempt
to create offspring before the impending tempeh
apocalypse. Sporulation also naturally occurs right before
tempeh becomes too mature. That's when you need to quickly
cool it.

   By creating ideal conditions, you let the molds grow
happily, live and let live, and then you cool, chill, or
freeze them to stop their growth at the most ideal state
for consumption.

NO GROWTH OR SPOTTY GROWTH

Having no *Rhizopus* mold growth can be linked to a variety
of things. Maybe the environment you've created for your
tempeh is too wet or too dry, maybe you undercooked the
beans, maybe the incubation chamber is too hot or cold.
These can all be factors in the fuzzy white tempeh mold
not growing.

OFF-SMELLS OR -FLAVORS

These are usually caused by undesirable bacteria wreaking
havoc. Slimy tempeh, ammonia or sulfur smells in your
tempeh, or other disgusting organoleptic cues are all
indicators that your tempeh is no good to eat. It probably
won't kill you, and it probably won't even make you sick,
but it certainly won't be delicious. Best to compost it
and start over.

OOH, YUMMY!

Symbiotic Colonies of Bacteria & Yeast

One of the things that I make the least but get the biggest thrill from is vinegar. The amount of time it generally takes to make a vinegar versus our high level of vinegar usage in the restaurant just doesn't math out well. I don't have enough time or room to age the amount of vinegar we go through. We use rivers of the stuff.

Most of the vinegars I do let myself make, therefore, go into specials or our retail bottles. I'm talking about traditional fruit-based vinegars as well as Kombucha Vinegar (page 112).

And while I don't get quite as much of a thrill from making kombucha, kefir, or ginger beer as I do from vinegar, the processes do have quite a bit of crossover. Lucky for me, I get to make those three fizzy ferments on a weekly basis. We produce about 40 gallons of kombucha, 20 gallons of water kefir, and 15 gallons of ginger beer every dang week. That's not a lot for a commercial brewery, but it'd sure as hell keep a home cook on their toes. The following recipes here, of course, are on the small-batch side for you. They're very easy to manage. Have fun!

Apple Cider Vinegar

****

1 quart plus 3 cups
   fresh-pressed apple
   cider or store-
   bought apple cider
Organic pure cane
   sugar, as needed
$^1/_4$ teaspoon yeast
   nutrient (available
   at homebrew supply
   shops and online)
$^1/_4$ teaspoon wine
   yeast, such as Red
   Star Côte des Blancs
$^3/_4$ cup raw
   unpasteurized apple
   cider vinegar with
   sediment, such as
   Bragg

****

MAKES 2 QUARTS

Before I started making my own vinegar, the most special vinegars to me were aged balsamics. When I had my first Portland restaurant, Portobello Vegan Trattoria, which started off moonlighting as a pop-up in my brother's coffee shop, I really came to appreciate them.

There was this wonderful married couple, two older men, who frequented Portobello from day one. For their 25th wedding anniversary, which they booked with us, I got them a really nice 25-year-aged balsamic. During their dinner, I came out from the kitchen and presented it to them. I said something like, "You've been in love for 25 years, when someone put this vinegar into its cask. Here's to you two, and to your beautiful love." It was a very sweet night for everyone.

Fast-forward to now, at Fermenter we make all sorts of seasonal fruit vinegars. I mean, we all make the occasional fruited vinegar at home when we leave a piece or two of past-its-prime fruit at the bottom of the fruit basket, right? Our Fermenter Apple Cider Vinegar is incredibly delicious, because we use the juice from special Pacific Northwest varieties that we adore, and we don't ferment them till they're bone-dry like store-bought cider vinegar. Those ones are predominantly sharp and harsh. Our apple cider vinegar has a very nice, ever so slightly sweet, full apple flavor to it. If you press your own cider for this, then please use a hydrometer (page 27) to measure its gravity.

1   If you are using your own fresh-pressed apple cider, then you'll want to use a hydrometer to take an original gravity reading (e.g., measure the sugar content) of your cider with it. You want the gravity to be 1.05 or higher. If the gravity is less than that, add 1 tablespoon of sugar to the juice at a time, stirring to dissolve, and then retest. Continue adding sugar until you've raised the gravity to 1.05.

2   Clean and sanitize your 2-quart jar and lid fitted with an airlock, and set both aside to air-dry.

3   Pour the cider into the jar, add the yeast nutrient, fasten the lid, and shake like crazy.

4   Remove the lid, add the wine yeast, and stir to combine. Wipe down the inside headspace of the jar, fasten the lid with the water-filled airlock, and set the cider aside to ferment at room temperature from 55 to 75 degrees F, and out of direct sunlight, for 1 to 2 weeks. It will get very bubbly and active in the beginning, and then it will slow down toward the end.

5   By the time you have to either shake the jar a bit or stand and stare at it for minutes at a time in order for it to bubble, it's time to open it up. Taste it. It should taste slightly alcoholic and quite dry. If it is, then add the raw, unpasteurized apple cider vinegar.

6   Cover the top of the jar with breathable cloth, secure it with twine or a rubber band, and continue to ferment at room temperature from 55 to 75 degrees F, and out of direct sunlight, for 1 to 2 months.

7   Every several days, using a clean spoon, give it a stir and taste it, and once it tastes tart and tasty and vinegary (see page 28 for more on pH), it's time to bottle and use. Vinegar keeps indefinitely.

8   If a SCOBY or mother has formed on the top of the vinegar, reserve it for your next batch of vinegar along with ¾ cup of the vinegar. If it hasn't, simply reserve ¾ cup of the vinegar if you want to start a new batch. That's your raw, unpasteurized apple cider vinegar for it.

NOTE: If the cider gets really active and seems like it might bubble out of the jar, you can always insert a tube into the jar where the airlock was and have that tube drop into another vessel. That way, the contents won't gush out like a cider volcano, and instead the cider will be routed into another container. Once fermentation slows down, you can combine them again in the original jar.

Persimmon Vinegar

YIELD: Well, that depends on your fruit!

The fun thing about persimmon vinegar is that everything
you need for the entire process is in or on the persimmons
from the very start. This is an unusual recipe, a really
soulful one, because we aren't giving you ingredient
amounts, volume, or even specific numbered steps. We're
just going to guide you through the process, which takes
two to three months. We want you to use your senses and
trust yourself. Let's jump off this dang persimmon
vinegar cliff together. I promise it'll be fun and very
much worth it.

   We were first inspired to make persimmon vinegar by
Sandor Katz and his 2021 book *Sandor Katz's Fermentation
Journeys: Recipes, Techniques, and Traditions from Around
the World*. Our version is a riff on his persimmon vinegar
recipe in that book. And Sandor's recipe is inspired by
recipes from Sharon Flynn, an Australian tour organizer,
and Nancy Singleton Hachisu, a Japan-based cookbook author
and food journalist. Ferments never exist alone. Recipes
never exist alone.

   If you live somewhere where the fall and winter can be
a bit of a slog—hello, Pacific Northwest!—this bright-
orange, full-of-life, go-with-the-flow persimmon vinegar
process, will feel really good on the darkest of days.
It's so nice to have something vibrant and colorful to
tend to then.

   Basically, get some persimmons once they're ripening
in the fall—fuyu persimmons (round and squat, like mini
pumpkins), not hachiya persimmons (more elongated, like
a plum tomato), not North American persimmons (small,
orangey-pink). Let them sit in a brown paper bag, rolled
up at the top, until they get very, very ripe—so ripe that
you are able to stick your finger through the skin and
into the flesh. They'll develop some dark spots, and some
will probably go bad as you wait it out. Be patient. Don't
be surprised if this takes a month or longer.

Once the persimmons are just about to collapse, remove and discard their brown crowns, and then put the persimmons into your fermentation container. Use whatever you have that's big enough and that you have an airlock, a wide-mouth jar, a food-grade bucket, a crock, etc. Whatever you use, you want it to be fairly wide at the top because vinegar needs and loves oxygen.

Mash the shit out of the persimmons in your vessel. Once you've done that, wipe down the inside walls. Put plastic wrap right over the top of the persimmons, and then top the vessel with your airlock.

Now simply let the natural yeasts on the persimmons—the wild yeasts—convert the sugars into alcohol and make everything nice and fizzy and boozy. After three weeks to one month, it should be boozy enough, and the fizziness should be subsiding as it runs out of sugars to ferment. The mash should be separating from the juice, and there should be a good amount of juice on the bottom of your vessel.

Open it up. Take the plastic wrap off and give it all a really good stir. After you've smelled all the good persimmon smells and stirred it up, you need to taste it and make sure that it's boozy. If you are sober, ask someone else to taste it for you. If it tastes alcoholic, congratulations, you've now graduated to phase two—daily stirring.

This is a good time to note that you should certainly feel free to use a hydrometer (page 27) to test the weight of the initial sugars here, and then later to test how much resulting alcohol there is. That said, people have been making vinegar this simple and soulful way around the world for ages without any tools like that. You can too. Think of this I-trust-you recipe as a way to synchronize yourself to the transformative power of microorganisms. The wild yeasts and wild acetic bacteria are all there. Rest assured, you're going to end up with vinegar.

From here on out, for about one additional month, stir
the persimmons a good deal every day. After you do so,
wipe down the insides of your vessel. You don't want molds
and yeasts to accumulate on the top of the persimmons.
If they do, just scrape them off and discard them. It's
really important to tend to the soon-to-be vinegar now,
and stir it often, because acetic acid loves oxygen.
You'll do this daily stirring, plus wiping down of the
vessel, until most of the alcohol has been converted to
acetic acid.

After the two to three months have passed since
starting your vinegar, and you have a nice acidic
persimmon vinegar, it's time to strain it. This will most
likely take a couple of days, because you need to weigh
down the thick fruit mash. We use big zip-top plastic bags
filled with water over perforated gastro pans. Whatever
you use, once you have your beautiful bright-orange
persimmon vinegar, strain it again and get rid of the
remaining sediment. Hello, persimmon vinegar!

Wintry salads go hand in hand with this vinegar that
you'll most likely start fermenting in the fall. When the
vinegar is done fermenting, after two to three months, you
can make a wintry salad with some sort of tasty combo—
maybe turnips, cabbages, pears, and/or apples? All year
round this vinegar is great with any salads that involve
deep greens like spinach and kale, crunchy radishes, and
other big bold veggies. It adds a lot of brightness and
beautiful flavor to whatever it graces.

I love that everything is here for you for this vinegar
from the very beginning. In and on the persimmons! It's
so freaking cool that the acetic bacteria and yeasts are
all there from get-go, just waiting to realize their full
potential. With your help, of course. Stirring, smelling,
straining, observing.

Botanical Kombucha

MAKES 13 CUPS, ABOUT 4 (750 ML) WINE BOTTLES

This is our all-time most popular kombucha at Fermenter. It's refreshingly bright and floral, and we brew and drink it year-round. I love that it tastes honeyed even though there isn't a drop of honey in it. It develops that really special, natural sweetness from all of the botanicals.

Making kombucha is fun. I love how day by day the SCOBY gets more and more buoyant and everything gets really active and effervescent. I also dig that it's fast enough to never be frustrating, and slow enough that you can control where you want it to go.

If you have any trouble sourcing the herbs or flowers here—there are quite a lot—I recommend checking out Mountain Rose Herbs (page 216) based in Eugene, Oregon. They're all about organic and sustainable, and all the other good stuff.

You can get this kombucha to a place of sourness and full flavor that you want to drink right away, you can bottle condition it till it's nice and fizzy, or you can let it go all the way acetic and turn it into a vinegar (page 112). So many options.

STEEP & INFUSE TAKES: ABOUT 2 HOURS
In a medium pot over high heat, bring 7 cups of the water to a boil, then remove from heat. Add the sugar and stir until dissolved. Combine the rose petals, hibiscus, sencha, verbena, chamomile, jasmine, lemon balm, lavender, and mint in a tea ball or sachet (don't pack it too tightly; you want the tea to be able to expand), and steep it in the water for about 1 hour.

Remove the tea ball or sachet, put it into another medium pot or pitcher, and pour the remaining 6 cups of cold water over it. Cold infuse the tea for about 1 hour.

BREW THE BOOCH TAKES: 3 TO 14 DAYS
Strain and pour both teas into a 1-gallon glass jar or other nonreactive 1-gallon vessel. Once the combined tea has cooled to 85 degrees F or cooler, add the SCOBY and starter kombucha.

CONTINUED

```
************************
13 cups water, divided
1 cup organic pure
   cane sugar
2 tablespoons dried
   rose petals
2 tablespoons dried
   hibiscus
1 tablespoon loose
   sencha tea, or 2 to
   3 tea bags
2 teaspoons dried
   verbena
1 teaspoon dried
   chamomile
1 teaspoon dried
   jasmine
1 teaspoon dried lemon
   balm
1 teaspoon dried
   lavender
1 teaspoon dried mint
Kombucha SCOBY (page
   19)
1¹/₂ cups starter
   kombucha (fully
   fermented kombucha
   from a previous
   batch or store
   bought)
************************
```

1

2

3

1   Brew your tea.

2   Add your SCOBY and
    starter booch.

3   Top it with breathable
    cloth and secure it.

4   Stir and taste it every
    day or so.

5   When you love it, strain
    it.

6   Bottle it and enjoy
    right away or bottle
    condition.

Cover the top of your fermentation vessel with breathable cloth, secure it with twine or a rubber band, and ferment it, out of direct sunlight, and at room temperature for 3 to 14 days. Kombucha is happiest when it's a warm 75 to 85 degrees F throughout fermentation. I tend to like small-batch kombucha, like this one, at 7 to 9 days in the fall and winter, and 5 to 7 days in the spring and summer.

Give it a stir and taste it every day or so, using a clean spoon. Once it tastes tart, tasty, and great to you, it's time to bottle.

BOTTLE TAKES: 5 TO 10 MINUTES
Remove the SCOBY along with 1½ cups of the kombucha. Put both into a clean jar and top it with breathable cloth, then secure it with twine or a rubber band, for your next batch of booch.

Strain the rest of the kombucha through a fine-mesh sieve or reusable coffee filter.

4   5   6

Funnel the kombucha into clean bottles (four securely fastened screw-cap wine bottles work great). Enjoy right away or refrigerate for up to 2 weeks. If you want fizzy kombucha then go ahead and bottle condition it; otherwise it's ready to drink. Generally, kombucha will not become fizzy once it is refrigerated because lactic acid fermentation slows way down in that temperature range.

BOTTLE CONDITION TAKES: 3 DAYS TO 1 WEEK
If you are looking for effervescence, bottle condition the kombucha for 3 days to 1 week, simply storing it at room temperature during this time. Again, that sweet spot of 75 to 85 degrees F is ideal. Keep an eye on your bottles throughout bottle conditioning because every batch is different, and you don't want any to explode. Once it is as effervescent as you like, enjoy some,and refrigerate the rest.

To ferment any excess kombucha into kombucha vinegar see page 112.

Beet-Ginger-Meyer Lemon Kombucha

****
13 cups water, divided
1 cup organic pure
   cane sugar
3 tablespoons loose
   sencha tea, or 6 to
   8 tea bags
Kombucha SCOBY (page
   19)
1¹/₂ cups starter
   kombucha (fully
   fermented kombucha
   from a previous
   batch or store
   bought)
¹/₂ cup ginger juice,
   or ¹/₂ cup minced
   unpeeled fresh
   ginger (see note)
1 cup beet juice,
   freshly juiced or
   store-bought
¹/₂ cup freshly
   squeezed Meyer lemon
   juice (about 2
   medium lemons)
****

MAKES 14½ TO 15 CUPS, ABOUT 5 (750 ML) WINE BOTTLES

I love this kombucha that's bright beet-red with a bit of Meyer lemon zing. I crave it. The ginger comes through, but it definitely doesn't overpower it. If you want to make this sencha kombucha with different fruit juices, store-bought or home-juiced, please do. Be creative and have fun. Simply use the same volume of juice—1½ cups total.

I guess it's a good time to say there really isn't any one fermentation vessel that trumps another when it comes to making kombucha. Basically, if you have a puddle of SCOBY in front of your home, and you add some kombucha starter and sweet tea to it, you'll end up with kombucha. For the slugs?

You can also get fancy and, oh, I don't know, brew your booch in hotel pans (shallow stainless pro-kitchen pans) like Noma in Copenhagen does? They do it that way to end up with more uniform rectangular SCOBYS afloat on top, which they then make into candies. For real. Check out their Insta. That's a much faster way to brew kombucha, by the way, because more of the tea is exposed to air.

STEEP & INFUSE TAKES: ABOUT 2 HOURS

In a medium pot over high heat, bring 7 cups of the water to a boil, and then remove from heat. Add the sugar and stir until dissolved. Add the tea (don't pack it too tightly if using a tea ball you want the tea to be able to expand) and steep it in the water for about 1 hour.

Remove the tea ball or tea bags, put them into another medium pot or pitcher, and pour the remaining 6 cups of cold water over them. Cold infuse the tea for about 1 hour.

> **NOTE:** If you plan to use minced ginger, as opposed to ginger juice, add it to the tea ball when steeping, then strain it out and discard it before adding the SCOBY. Or leave it in and have a ginger SCOBY!

BREW THE BOOCH TAKES: 3 TO 14 DAYS
Follow steps on page 107.

ADD JUICE & BOTTLE TAKES: 5 TO 10 MINUTES
Remove the SCOBY along with 1½ cups of the kombucha. Put both into a clean jar and top it with breathable cloth, then secure it with twine or a rubber band for your next batch of booch.

Strain the rest of the kombucha through a fine-mesh sieve or reusable coffee filter.

If you used minced ginger, discard it. Add the beet juice, Meyer lemon juice, and ginger juice (if you did not use minced ginger), and stir to combine.

Funnel the kombucha into clean bottles (five securely fastened screw-cap wine bottles work great). Enjoy right away or refrigerate for up to 2 weeks. If you want fizzy kombucha then go ahead and bottle condition it, otherwise it's ready to drink. Generally, kombucha will not become fizzy once it is refrigerated because lactic acid fermentation slows way down in that temperature range.

BOTTLE CONDITION TAKES: 3 DAYS TO 1 WEEK
Follow steps on page 109.

Kombucha Vinegar

Kombucha vinegar is a really cool way to make easy-peasy vinegar at home. Do you have so much booch brewed that you won't be able to drink it all? Pour it into whatever clean jar it fits in with at least 1 inch of headspace. Top the jar with a lightweight breathable cloth, and secure it with twine or a rubber band. Now pretty much leave it alone beyond giving it a stir every once in a while. Before you know it, you'll have a really cool vinegar.

You'll also have zero waste. It's such a bummer when folks toss kombucha. Take the end of any bottle of booch (or even any glass of it, if that doesn't gross you out), and start collecting. In general, it takes 3 to 6 weeks of room-temperature fermentation for your booch to transform into a tasty ready-to-use vinegar, in the 1.8 to 2.5 pH range. Taste it as you go.

Whenever we bottle kombucha at Fermenter, we have a collection pan underneath the bottles. When we're done bottling, we pour all of that mix-and-match booch into a big-ass jar and we ferment it into vinegar.

You don't need to add a vinegar mother or kombucha SCOBY to it. With kombucha vinegar, the booch SCOBY just keeps on consuming sugars, and turning that into alcohol, while simultaneously turning the alcohol into acetic acid. All the microorganisms work around the clock until the kombucha is dry. They hustle on overtime to make you the most delicious KOMBUCHA VINEGAR!

Ginger Beer

MAKES 7 CUPS

Mainstream big-brand ginger ales have very little ginger in them, while ours is pretty dang flavorful. You can always increase or decrease the ginger content here to your taste. Start with a cup of chopped fresh ginger and see how you like it.

DAYS ONE THROUGH FIVE

Start by making the ginger bug at least a week before (page 114).

DAY FIVE

In a small pot over high heat, bring 2 cups of the water to a boil, and then remove from heat. Add ½ cup of the sugar and stir until dissolved. Add the remaining 5 cups of water and cool the mix to room temperature.

Add 1 cup of the unstrained ginger bug's liquid (no need to strain out the minced ginger in it) with the 1 cup of ginger to a blender. Puree it for 10 to 15 seconds until the ginger is roughly minced.

Transfer the blended gingery liquid to a large gallon jar along with the room-temperature sugar water. Stir it up. Time to start fermenting!

Feed your ginger bug with 1 cup of this unstrained ginger beer mix to keep your ginger bug active. Replace the covering on your happily fed ginger bug. Cover the top of the ginger beer jar with breathable cloth, and secure it with twine or a rubber band.

DAYS SIX TO ELEVEN

Ferment it, out of direct sunlight, and at room temperature for 5 to 7 days. Once fully fermented, it will be gingery and dry.

Strain the ginger beer through a fine-mesh sieve into a large pitcher.

DAY TWELVE AND BEYOND

Stir in the remaining ½ cup of sugar. Add the strained ginger to your ginger bug.

To bottle condition, transfer the ginger beer to clean bottles.

Bottle condition the ginger beer for 2 days to 1 week at room temperature. Keep an eye on it during this time, because every batch is different, and you don't want any exploding bottles. Once it is as effervescent as you like, enjoy some, and refrigerate the rest for up to 2 weeks.

```
*********************
7 cups water, divided
1 cup organic pure
  cane sugar, divided
1 cup ginger bug
  (recipe follows)
1 cup unpeeled roughly
  chopped fresh ginger
*********************
```

CONTINUED

Ginger Bug

MAKES ABOUT 3 CUPS

A ginger bug is basically just ginger, water, sugar plus time. You have to take care of it, just like with any perpetual culture. Trust me, it's worth it. Oh, and I don't know why the heck it's called a ginger bug. FYI, I've never seen it crawling on the counter.

****
2 cups water
2 tablespoons organic
   pure cane sugar
2 tablespoons unpeeled,
   minced fresh ginger
****

****
¹/₂ cup plus 2
   tablespoons organic
   pure cane sugar,
   divided
³/₄ cup plus 3
   tablespoons
   unpeeled, minced
   fresh ginger,
   divided
****

****
Additional organic
   pure cane sugar and
   unpeeled, minced
   fresh ginger to be
   added as needed
****

DAY ONE

In a small pot over high heat, heat the water and sugar, stirring regularly, just until the sugar is completely dissolved. Remove from heat and cool to room temperature.

Add the ginger to a quart jar and pour the room-temperature sugar water over it. Cover the jar with a lid and set aside at room temperature for 1 day.

DAYS TWO THROUGH SIX

Add 2 tablespoons organic pure cane sugar and 3 tablespoons ginger daily, stirring the bug when you do, and then fasten the lid. After 4 to 5 days, when the ginger bug smells a bit yeasty and is fizzy, it's ready to use.

Remove the lid, and cover the top of your ginger bug jar with breathable cloth. Secure it with twine or a rubber band, and keep it out of direct sunlight and at room temperature.

DAY SEVEN AND BEYOND

From here on out, you'll maintain your ginger bug alongside your ginger beer. Your batch of ginger beer will be made from part of your ginger bug, and a portion of the ginger beer will also go back into your ginger bug to feed it. Round and round. You know that song from Ratt?

If you aren't going to make a batch of ginger beer for a while, go ahead and lid and refrigerate it. Feed it roughly 2 tablespoons of sugar and 2 tablespoons of minced ginger a week until you use it again.

Blueberry-Lemon Balm Ginger Beer

MAKES 2 QUARTS

When I was little, ginger beer, more commonly known as ginger ale, was my airplane sipper of choice. Kids everywhere can relate to this. I'm guessing it stems from moms and pops telling their kids to drink it then to settle their little tum-tums. Ginger is definitely good for the gut.

At Fermenter, we almost always have a fruited ginger beer in the cold case. We make peach-ginger beer, rhubarb-grapefruit ginger beer, and of course, this one. If you don't have blueberries feel free to substitute the same amount of another yummy fruit shrub. You can also add juices, fresh and dried fruits, flowers and herbs etc.

DAY ONE TO TWO
Make the Blueberry–Lemon Balm Shrub (page 117).

DAY THREE AND BEYOND
Follow the Ginger Beer recipe (page 113) through to Day 12. Do not add that ½ cup of sugar that our straight-up Ginger Beer calls for. You'll get that sweetness here from the shrub.

Before bottling, in a gallon jar add the unstrained Blueberry–Lemon Balm Shrub to the Ginger Beer. Using an immersion blender, if you have one, blend the mix for 15 to 20 seconds. This infuses the ginger beer with even more flavor. If you don't have an immersion blender it is perfectly fine to skip this step. Top the jar with a lid, and refrigerate for 2 days.

To bottle condition, using a fine-mesh sieve, strain the fruited ginger beer (discard the fruit, or save it for a yummy quick jam), and transfer it to clean bottles—three screw-cap wine bottles work great. You'll end up with some fruit pulp in your ginger beer this way. I like it that way, but if you don't, line your sieve with a double layer of cheesecloth before straining.

Bottle condition the ginger beer for 2 days to 1 week, at room temperature, in order to get it nice and bubbly. Keep an eye on your bottles throughout bottle conditioning because every batch is different, and you don't want any exploding bottles. Once it is as effervescent as you like, enjoy some and refrigerate the rest for up to 2 weeks.

CONTINUED

```
***********************
1 batch of Ginger Beer
  to Day 12 (page 113)
1¹/₂ cups unstrained
  Blueberry-Lemon
  Balm Shrub (recipe
  follows)
***********************
```

Blueberry–Lemon Balm Shrub

MAKES 1 CUP IF STRAINED, ABOUT 1½ CUPS IF NOT

If you make this tasty and beautiful shrub for our ginger beer, I highly recommend saving the leftover blueberries from the shrub mash and cooking them down with a little bit of sugar into a quick and delicious Blueberry–Lemon Balm jam. If you decide to go that jam route, you might want to add the lemon balm to the ginger beer shrub in a sachet so that you can discard it at the end before moving on to making the jam.

DAY ONE

In a medium bowl, stir together the blueberries and sugar. Add the lemon balm. Stir to incorporate, and mash up the berries a bit. Cover the bowl with a towel or lid, and let sit overnight (12 or more hours).

DAY TWO

Stir in the vinegar, and let sit overnight (an additional 12 or more hours).

DAY THREE

The shrub is now ready to add to the ginger beer as is, or you can strain and store it. If you would like to strain the shrub, line a colander or fine-mesh sieve with cheesecloth, and place it over a bowl.

Transfer the shrub to it, and let it drain for about 30 minutes. Do not press on it during this time, but gently stir now and again.

Once the shrub has completely drained, use it or bottle and refrigerate it, for up to 1 month.

```
************************
6 ounces blueberries
   (about 1 heaping
   cup)
1/2 cup organic pure
   cane sugar
1/3 cup stemmed and
   chopped fresh lemon
   balm
1/2 cup plus 1
   tablespoon white
   wine vinegar
************************
```

Water Kefir

****
2 tablespoons, plus
  2 teaspoon organic
  pure cane sugar
2 tablespoons, plus
  2 teaspoon finely
  chopped panela
  (unrefined whole
  cane sugar that
  often comes in small
  light brown cones,
  discs, or blocks
  from Central and
  Latin America, or
  loose and bagged in
  grocery stores)
2 quarts water
¹/₂ cup hydrated water
  kefir grains
****

MAKES ABOUT 2 QUARTS

Once you get the hang of making our nicely effervescent water kefir, it's so much fun because you can turn around a yummy, fizzy kefir drink in just a couple days. An added bonus to making our water kefir is that you can then make all our cheeses. A small amount of water kefir goes into all of them.

If this is your first time using water kefir grains that you've rehydrated, it'll most likely take a few batches before they're in the full swing of things and fermenting water kefir properly. Don't give up!

For water kefir, you want a certain level of mineral content and little to no chlorine. You also need to feed kefir grains regularly. If you don't, you'll most likely end up with cheesy kefir—yeasty and funky smelling and tasting. If your water kefir grains that smell like that, I'm sorry, I don't know a consistent fix. Either try a technique listed below for adding minerality, research other techniques, or simply send them to the compost, and get yourself some new grains.

DAY ONE
In a 1-gallon glass jar or other nonreactive fermentation vessel, add the sugar, panela, and water and stir with a nonreactive spoon until the sugars have dissolved.

Add the hydrated kefir grains to the jar or vessel. Cover the jar in a breathable cloth, and secure it with twine or a rubber band.

DAYS TWO TO SIX
Place the jar in a 70 to 80 degree F spot, out of direct sunlight, and ferment for 2 to 4 days, until it has filled out a bit in flavor. It'll be a bit sour, and it might have a tiny bit of effervescence.

DAY SIX AND BEYOND
Strain the sugar water and kefir grains through a fine plastic strainer into a clean 1-gallon jar. Sometimes water kefir grains are so fine that you won't want to strain them. Other times, they will be plump and easy to strain. If they are too fine to strain, simply pour the water kefir off carefully from the top and retain the settled water kefir grains at the bottom of the jar.

Proceed with the recipe for Raspberry–Lime Leaf Kefir (page 121), and either store the water kefir grains for future use (page 120), or start a new batch. Do one or the other in order to maintain the health and vibrancy of your water kefir grains.

CONTINUED

1

2

3

4

1   Feed and maintain your kefir grains.

2   Strain the kefir from the water kefir grains.

3   Add your shrub to the strained water kefir.

4   Store your kefir grains.

NOTE: We've found that water kefir grains prefer a nice 70 and 80 degrees F, to be harvested and re-fed regularly, and a good amount of minerals. By adding organic pure cane sugar and mineral-rich panela, you give the grains all the nutrients they need to grow up big and strong. Watch your grains multiply, and prepare to start making bigger batches and handing out kefir starters to all your buddies.

STORING WATER KEFIR GRAINS

Up to 1 month: Transfer the grains to a quart jar. Dissolve 2 tablespoons sugar and 2 tablespoons panela in 3 cups of water, cover, and refrigerate. When ready to use again, bring the jar to room temperature, strain the grains (drink the storage liquid if it smells good and you want to), and proceed.

Longer than 1 month: Rinse the grains with water, and then dehydrate at room temperature for a few days, or in a dehydrator set to low until fully dry. Refrigerate the dried grains in an airtight container. When ready to use again, rehydrate as you did originally. You can also strain the water kefir grains and freeze them in an airtight container up to 3 months. When ready to use again, defrost them to room temperature and proceed.

Raspberry-Lime Leaf Kefir

MAKES 2 QUARTS

I've had some water kefirs that are really funky and dry over the years. Ours are a bit sweeter, including this tasty seasonal raspberry one, and in my opinion much more drinkable. Getting started with water kefir, if you haven't fermented it before, requires a little TLC. To start, you'll want to use nonreactive tools and vessels—wooden, plastic, or glass—because kefir grains often get irritated when they come into contact with metal. So go ahead and get out a 1-gallon glass jar, wooden spoon, and a fine plastic strainer.

DAYS ONE THROUGH THREE

Make the Raspberry–Lime Leaf Shrub and brew the water kefir. Follow the steps for the Water Kefir recipe until it is fully fermented after 2 to 4 days and you've strained out the water kefir grains.

DAYS FOUR TO SIX

Add the unstrained Raspberry–Lime Leaf Shrub (page 122) to the strained Water Kefir (page 118) in your clean 1-gallon jar. Using an immersion blender, if you have one, blend the mix for 15 to 20 seconds, in order to chop up the fruit and lime leaf a bit more in order to infuse more flavor. If you don't have an immersion blender, it is perfectly fine to skip this step. Top with a lid, and refrigerate for 2 days.

DAY SEVEN AND BEYOND

To bottle condition, using a fine plastic strainer, strain the fruited water kefir (discard the fruit, or save it for a yummy quick jam, see page 122), and transfer it into clean bottles—three screw-cap wine bottles work great. You'll end up with some fruit pulp in your kefir this way. I like it that way, but if you don't, then line your sieve with a double layer of cheesecloth before straining.

Bottle condition the kefir for 2 days to 1 week, at room temperature, in order to get it nice and bubbly. That sweet spot of 70 to 80 degrees F is ideal. Keep an eye on your bottles throughout bottle conditioning because every batch is different, and you don't want exploding bottles. Once it is as effervescent as you like, enjoy some and refrigerate the rest for up to 2 weeks.

CONTINUED

****

$^1/_2$ cup organic pure cane sugar

2 tablespoons finely chopped panela (unrefined whole cane sugar that often comes in small light-brown cones, discs, or blocks from Central and Latin America, or loose and bagged in grocery stores)

2 quarts water, divided

$^1/_4$ to $^1/_2$ cup hydrated water kefir grains

$1^1/_2$ cups unstrained Raspberry-Lime Leaf Shrub (recipe follows)

****

Note: If you make this water kefir, I highly recommend saving the leftover raspberries from the shrub mash and cooking them down with a bit of sugar into a quick and delicious raspberry–lime leaf jam. If you decide to go that jam route, simply add the lime leaf to the water kefir shrub in a sachet so that you can discard it at the end before moving on to making the jam.

Raspberry–Lime Leaf Shrub
MAKES 1 CUP IF STRAINED, ABOUT 1 ½ CUPS IF NOT

****
6 ounces (about 1
  heaping cup) golden
  raspberries, or red
  raspberries
$^1/_2$ cup plus 1
  tablespoon organic
  pure cane sugar
3 lime leaves
$^1/_2$ cup plus 1
  tablespoon white
  wine vinegar
****

We love adding all sorts of flavor bases to our water kefir, in addition to this raspberry–lime leaf shrub. A rainbow of flavors really opens up your kefir options like at an Italian soda counter. You can add all sorts of things to water kefir including juices, shrubs, fresh and dried fruits, flowers and herbs, coconut water, etc. I just recommend that you add your flavoring once you've completed your base water kefir, strained off the kefir grains, and set them aside for your next batch. Flavorings can damage the sensitive grains.

DAY ONE
In a medium bowl, stir together the raspberries and sugar. By hand, roughly tear the lime leaves, and add them to the bowl. Stir to incorporate, and mash up the berries a bit. Cover the bowl with a towel or lid, and let sit overnight (12 or more hours).

DAY TWO
Stir in the vinegar, and let sit overnight (an additional 12 or more hours).

DAY THREE
It's now ready to add to the water kefir as is, or you can strain and store it. If you would like to strain the shrub, line a colander or fine-mesh sieve with cheesecloth, and place it over a bowl.

Transfer the shrub to it, and let it drain for about 30 minutes. Do not press on it during this time, but gently stir now and again.

Once the shrub has completely drained, use it or bottle and refrigerate it, for up to 1 month.

1

2

3

4

1   Add the shrub to the strained water kefir.

2   Stir it up.

3   Strain the fruited water kefir.

4   Bottle and then bottle condition it.

Vegan Dairy:

YOU'RE NOT FOOLING ANYONE

When I first took a crack at making vegan cheese, I tried my best to make cheeses that were like the ones I ate as an omnivore. The only thing that helped make them taste anything close to real dairy cheese was time. That is, enough time for me to actually forget what dairy cheese tasted like. So I gave up. And from that surrender came something wonderful.

The goal of vegan cheese and dairy should not be to create an analog of animal-based cheese and dairy, but to make something that serves the same purpose with its own unique and distinctive character. A cheese made of hazelnuts, sunflower seeds, oats, or whatever, is never going to taste like a Roquefort, Comté, Emmental, or Cotija. It just isn't. And that's OK. Let's please have our own special thing.

If you decide to make vegan cheeses often, I highly recommend investing in a Vitamix or another high-powered blender (page 29). If you don't use one for them, sooner or later (and I'm guessing sooner) you'll blow out your blender.

The All-Seeing Eye

The first time it occurred to me to become vegetarian was
when I moved to a new house in California in the sixth
grade. Our previous house had burned down that year, and
we ended up living in a hotel for a few months. Family
photos are one of the things that make me the saddest
about that fire. We hardly have any. I think I was a kid
once? I'm pretty sure I was.

   So we moved to a new house. One thing that made it out
of the fire, with just some charring on the top, was this
mirrored armoire of my mom's. You know how old furniture
sometimes gets a little out of plumb and is no longer
exactly straight? That's how this armoire was. The door
simply would not stay closed. We set it down when we were
moving in, and the door creaked open right in front of my
face. Suddenly the mirror was right in front of me. I can
remember exactly how the light was in the room at that
moment, as it came through the window. I could see my eyes
dilating in the mirror.

   I thought, holy shit, I'm alive! It dawned on me in a
really intense way, at that very moment, just how amazing
life is. It really affected me. I don't know exactly what
it was, but at that moment I thought, whoa, look at how
this thing called life works! And then, of course, I saw
the same eyes on other animals. I thought, yeah, I don't
think I'm going to participate in that anymore, in eating
animals, in killing them.

   Becoming a vegetarian got me interested in cooking,
because suddenly I had to cook for myself. My mom was

like, "So is pork vegetarian?" It was tough for my family
to understand. But ultimately my mom was pretty cool about
it, and she'd take me to the local health food store to
pick up tofu, soy milk, and stuff like that. I ate cheese,
but only rennetless or vegetable rennet cheese.

I stayed vegetarian from sixth grade until the end of
my senior year in 1993 that first time. My mom had moved
to Washington, and I was still in high school. I was
hanging out with my friend Joe and we were at a punk show
at Gilman Street. I was wasted, and all of the sudden I
thought, Do I even care about being vegetarian anymore?
At that point, I was just doing it because I'd decided to
years prior.

So I left the show, and went and got myself a can of
Dinty Moore beef ravioli. I ate it all up. And then I
threw it all up pretty quickly. I'm sorry. That was when
I started eating meat, seafood, and dairy again, until
I became vegan again in 2002 right before I moved to
Portland. I think my very young self thought that being
a vegetarian would hold me back in the world of cooking.
And, you know, I feel pretty conflicted saying it, but
young me was probably right. At that time, there weren't a
lot of rad vegetarian restaurants. Younger Aaron would be
so stoked to see the number of amazing vegan restaurants
around today. From local faves like Obon Shokudo,
Mirisata, and Boxcar Pizza to international sensation
Eleven Madison Park, we're certainly blessed. I can only
dream of coming up a cook in this day and age.

Sunflower Yogurt

****
4 cups raw hulled
  sunflower seeds
  (about 1¹/₄ pound),
  or the same volume
  of raw hazelnuts
  (about 1 pound), see
  note
¹/₄ cup gluten-free
  traditional oats
6 cups water, divided,
  plus more for
  boiling
¹/₈ teaspoon vegan
  yogurt culture (page
  22)
¹/₂ teaspoon finely
  chopped panela (see
  note), or organic
  pure cane sugar
¹/₄ teaspoon Water
  Kefir (page 118)
****

NOTE: Panela is
unrefined whole cane
sugar that often comes
in small light brown
cones, discs, or blocks
from Central and Latin
America, or loose and
bagged in grocery
stores.

MAKES ABOUT 1 QUART

Our yogurt is a lot like our cheeses in terms of process, but it has different ingredients and proportions and, of course, we use a vegan yogurt culture to get it going. This yogurt goes into so many different things at Fermenter including our Ranch Dressing (page 199), our garlicky Yogurt Sauce (page 193) for the Fermenter Bowl, and as a topper for our Cheesy Jojo Supreme with Tempeh Bacon (page 183). I also love to make a tasty parfait with it. Got some seeds, nuts, and fruit? Great! Make a layered parfait with this yogurt and start your day off right.

NOTE: If you have hazelnuts and want to make hazelnut yogurt instead, simply use the same amount (4 cups) as the sunflower seeds, but process them as you do for the Kefir-Cultured Hazelnut Cheese Base in terms of blanching, removing skins, and boiling them (pages 133–134). Increase the baking soda to 1½ teaspoons when following those steps.

PREPARE THE SUNFLOWER SEEDS & OATS TAKES: 30 TO 40 MINUTES
Fill a large pot three-quarters full with water and bring to a boil over high heat. Once boiling, add the sunflower seeds and cook for 10 minutes. Drain them in a colander, reserving ½ cup of the boiled water for the oats, and rinse with cold water.

Meanwhile, put the oats in a medium bowl, and pour the ½ cup of boiling water over them. Stir well, cover, and hydrate the oats for 20 to 30 minutes.

BLEND & STRAIN TAKES: 30 TO 40 MINUTES
In the bowl of a high-powered blender, add half the seeds, all the oats, 3 cups of the water and blend, starting at low and slowly increasing to high, for 5 to 7 minutes until completely smooth. It will get quite warm as it blends and that's OK.

Strain the sunflower seed milk through a fine-mesh sieve in several batches, using a soft spatula to push it through, into a medium heavy-bottomed pot.

Repeat the blending of the remaining sunflower seeds and 3 cups of the water, and once smooth, push it through the sieve into the pot.

You will discard some very thick portions from each sieve-worth, about 1 cup total.

COOK TAKES: ABOUT 2 HOURS
Transfer the pot to medium heat and cook for 8 to 10 minutes, stirring constantly to avoid scorching, until the milk is 180 degrees F and just starting to simmer.

Transfer the hot sunflower seed milk to a large bowl, set aside, and cool until an instant-read thermometer registers 108 degrees F.

CULTURE & INCUBATE TAKES: 24 TO 48 HOURS
Add the vegan yogurt culture, panela, and Water Kefir, and stir to combine.

Transfer the yogurt mix to two (1-quart) jars, top them with breathable cloth, and secure with twine or a rubber band.

Put the yogurt jars into your warm incubator (page 80) that's between 108 and 112 degrees F, and incubate them for 24 hours. If you can set an exact incubation temperature, set it to 108 degrees F.

After 24 hours, taste the yogurt. It should have a nice sunflower seed taste and be smooth and tangy.

If it is to your liking, then proceed to the next step. If not, remove it from the incubator and set it on the countertop, at room temperature, for up to 24 more hours, or until it is sour and tasty.

DRAIN TAKES: 12 OR MORE HOURS
Set a colander over a large bowl, and line the colander with a triple layer of cheesecloth. Use a spatula to gently transfer the yogurt to the cheesecloth-lined colander, then cover the colander and bowl with plastic wrap or a lid.

Transfer the colander/bowl to the refrigerator and let the mix drain overnight (12 or more hours), until it is nice and thick like a proper yogurt. If your colander does not sit fairly high above the bowl, you might want to empty the bowl's whey into a jar, to save it, once or twice. You don't want the yogurt to sit on the whey.

CONTINUED

You will end up with 1 cup or more of whey, which keeps for roughly 2 to 3 months. I highly recommend that you save it and use it; see note below.

Once it's done draining, enjoy the yogurt right away, or contain and refrigerate for up to 2 weeks.

NOTE: Consider salting the whey and using it as a brine for sunflower-whey-brined vegetable pickles! You'll probably want to add 2 percent salt by weight to it if you go that route. Simply use it like you do the brine for our Sour Dills (page 39) and submerge your veggies in it.

Kefir-Cultured Hazelnut Cheese Base

MAKES 4 ⅓ TO 4½ CUPS

We use Water Kefir to culture this cheese base because we like wild cheesemaking. It delivers the ideal flavor, acidity, and butteriness for all the cheeses you make with it. Whip up this base recipe, cure it in a 2-quart jar, and then go on to make tubs of our Creamy Kefir Cheese (page 137), the Cheese Sauce Situation (page 184), our Wine-Washed Aged Cheese (page 141), or mix and match. All of this chapter's recipes are modular and versatile.

Maybe dive right in with a full batch of an aged cheese? Both of those recipes make three small wheels. Then you can use the remaining base for a mini tub of Creamy Kefir Cheese. Best of both worlds. Either wash the aged cheese wheels with wine (or beer, cider, pickle brine . . .) like a true-blue affineur (page 141), or roll them in herbs and spices (page 146) and enjoy.

VARIATION: Cashew-Hazelnut Cheese Base. For creamier cheeses, add cashews. Use 1¾ cups of hazelnuts prepared in the same way as the hazelnut cheese base, but with just ¾ teaspoon of baking soda and 1½ cups cashews. Fill a medium pot three-quarters full with water, and bring to a boil over high heat. Once boiling, remove from heat and add the cashews to the pot. Soak them in water for 20 to 30 minutes, until the water has cooled to warm. Drain the cashews in a colander, and set aside.

VARIATION: Sunflower Seed Cheese Base. If you'd like to make a sunflower seed cheese base instead of hazelnut or cashew, because of a nut allergy or to cut cost, simply use the same volume of sunflower seeds as hazelnuts. Rinse the 3¼ cups of sunflower seeds and then boil them for 10 minutes in water. Omit the baking soda, washing, and skin peeling.

PREPARE THE HAZELNUTS & OATS TAKES: ABOUT 1 HOUR
Fill a large pot three-quarters full with water and the baking soda, and bring to a boil over high heat. Then once boiling, add the hazelnuts and cook for 5 minutes.

Drain them in a colander, and rinse with cold water.

```
************************
1¹/₄ teaspoon baking
   soda
3¹/₄ cups raw hazelnuts
¹/₄ cup gluten-free
   traditional oats
1 tablespoon Water
   Kefir (page 118)
0.5 percent sea salt
   by weight, or 1
   teaspoon
************************
```

CONTINUED

1

2

3

1   Blend the boiled
    hazelnuts and oats.

2   Add the water kefir.

3   Transfer to ripen in a
    2-quart jar.

4   Strain in a colander
    over a large bowl for 3
    to 4 days for the Creamy
    Kefir Cheese (page 137).

5   Fold in desired herbs,
    jams, or ferments (pages
    138-139) for various
    flavored Creamy Kefir
    cheeses.

6   Enjoy the heck out of
    it!

Using your fingers, a large bowl of water, and a towel, peel off the hazelnut skins. They should come off fairly easily, but it certainly is tedious. Roughly rub them between your hands in the water, moving your hands back and forth like you're trying to warm your hands up. Use the towel to push/peel them off as well. Once the majority of hazelnuts are peeled, rinse them with cold water and set aside.

Fill a large pot three-quarters full with water, and bring to a boil over high heat. Then once boiling, add the peeled hazelnuts and cook for 20 minutes. Drain them in a colander, and set aside to cool to room temperature.

Meanwhile, put the oats in a medium bowl and pour ½ cup of boiling water over them. Stir well, cover, and hydrate the oats for 20 to 30 minutes.

NOTE: At Fermenter, we do much bigger batches, so we take a garden hose with a special nozzle and high-pressure spray the hazelnut skins off in a pasta basket.

BLEND & CULTURE TAKES: ABOUT 15 MINUTES

In the bowl of a high-powered blender (page 29), add the hazelnuts (and cashews if using), along with 2¼ cups water, and blend, starting at low and slowly increasing the speed to medium, for 5 to 6 minutes, or until smooth.

Add the oats and blend for 4 to 5 more minutes, until smooth and creamy.

Transfer the cheese base to a large bowl, and cool until an instant-read thermometer registers below 110 degrees F.

Add the Water Kefir and salt, and stir well to incorporate.

4
5
6

RIPEN TAKES: 3 DAYS OR MORE

Pour the mixture into a 2-quart glass jar, cover it in breathable cloth, and secure it with twine or a rubber band.

Place the jar in a warm spot to ripen.

After 1 to 2 days, it should be active and creating air bubbles. Check on it every day. If there is mold on top, scrape it off and discard it.

After 2 to 3 days, taste it. It should be thick and creamy and a bit tangy (right around 4.5 pH) with some light buttery tones.

If it is tangy, but there aren't enough cheesy/buttery tones, move the mixture to a cooler spot (an air-conditioned room, your refrigerator) and ripen a bit longer. The cooler the temperature at which you ripen it, the longer it will take.

MAKE CREAMY KEFIR CHEESE OR AGED CHEESE

Once the flavor of your cheese base is ideal, either proceed to make cheese or keep it lidded and refrigerated for up to 2 weeks. You can use this base to make some sweet and/or savory spreadable Creamy Kefir Cheese (page 137), one of our more refined deep and tangy aged cheeses (pages 141-146) (similar to a semi-firm aged goat cheese), or both. This recipe will make three aged wheels (with 3⅓ cups) and with the remaining roughly 1 cup of base you can make 1 mini tub of Creamy Kefir Cheese. Add ¼ teaspoon of salt to the mini tub of Creamy Kefir Cheese, rather than the called-for 1 teaspoon and proceed with the Creamy Kefir Cheese recipe.

Creamy Kefir Cheese

MAKES 3 (1-CUP) TUBS

Our Creamy Kefir Cheese is super popular at Fermenter. Think of it as a versatile semi-sour spreadable cheesy thing that you can add all sorts of sweet and savory components to—like herbs, spices, shallots, kraut, pickles, and jams—making it into a delicious spread or dip. On its own it's much closer to a soft sheep or goat milk cheese than to a cheese. It's nice and bright.

First you make the Kefir-Cultured Hazelnut Cheese Base (page 133), then season it and drain it, and finally, if you want, you fold in savory or sweet components of choice. The Chive Creamy Kefir Cheese is our #1 selling cheese.

Spread some Chive Creamy Kefir Cheese on a summery tempeh bacon and tomato sandwich and you won't regret it. Or make the Jammy Creamy Kefir Cheese (page 139), and swirl it into a yummy morning spread for toast. Or just enjoy the plain Creamy Kefir straight up! We love all of these super spreaders (sorry, COVID, had to) on bagels, in wraps, on melts, on toast, and with chips and crackers. Have fun with it. We do.

MAKE THE CHEESE BASE TAKES: 3 DAYS TO 4 DAYS
Make the Kefir-Cultured Hazelnut Cheese Base.

> **NOTE:** In terms of yield, from 4⅓ to 4½ cups of Kefir-Cultured Hazelnut Cheese Base you will end up with 2½ to 3 cups of drained Creamy Kefir Cheese.

STRAIN THE CHEESE TAKES: 3 DAYS TO 4 DAYS
Add 1 teaspoon of fine sea salt. Stir until well incorporated.

Set a colander over a large bowl, and line the colander with a double layer of cheesecloth. Pour the cheese base into the cheesecloth-lined colander, then cover the colander and bowl with plastic wrap.

Transfer the colander/bowl to the refrigerator and let it drain for 3 to 4 days. At this point it will have thickened and will be nicely acidic with light cheesy tones.

CONTINUED

FLAVOR THE CHEESE TAKES: 5 TO 10 MINUTES

Taste, then add more salt if desired and enjoy as is. Or carry on and add yummy things to it for our Chive Creamy Kefir Cheese, Shallot & Herbs Creamy Kefir Cheese, Jammy Creamy Kefir Cheese, Krauty Creamy Kefir Cheese, or Pickley Creamy Kefir Cheese (recipes follow).

> **NOTE:** Don't discard the accumulated liquid from straining. It's hazelnut whey! Use it in our Sunshine Cookies (page 205)! There is way more whey (hardy har) produced in the yogurt recipe, but you can still use the small amount you end up with here.

Chive Creamy Kefir Cheese
ABOUT 1 CUP

```
**********************
1 cup strained Creamy
  Kefir Cheese (page
  137)
1/4 cup finely sliced
  fresh chives
Kosher salt
**********************
```

In a small bowl, fold the chives into the Creamy Kefir Cheese. Salt to taste.

Serve right away, or transfer to a lidded container and refrigerate up to 1 week.

Shallot & Herbs Creamy Kefir Cheese
ABOUT 1 CUP

```
**********************
1 teaspoon extra-
  virgin olive oil
2 medium shallots,
  finely minced
2 teaspoons stemmed
  and minced fresh
  thyme
2 teaspoons minced
  fresh chives
2 teaspoons stemmed
  and minced fresh
  flat-leaf parsley
1 cup drained Creamy
  Kefir Cheese (page
  137)
Kosher salt
**********************
```

In a small pan over medium heat, add the olive oil and saute the shallots for a few minutes until cooked, then set aside. In a small bowl, fold the minced thyme, chives, and parsley into the Creamy Kefir Cheese, and then add the cooled shallot. Salt to taste.

Serve right away, or transfer to a lidded container and refrigerate up to 1 week.

Jammy Creamy Kefir Cheese
ABOUT 1 CUP

In a small bowl, swirl the jam into the Creamy Kefir Cheese.

Serve right away, or transfer to a lidded container and refrigerate for 1 to 2 days.

> **NOTE:** Jam is better than fresh fruit here because the cheese has a very short shelf life when married with fresh fruit. Sugar activates the cheese, and it will quickly over-ferment.

```
**********************
1 cup drained Creamy
  Kefir Cheese (page
  137)
3 tablespoons your
  preferred jam
**********************
```

Krauty Creamy Kefir Cheese
ABOUT 1 CUP

In a small bowl, fold the kraut into the Creamy Kefir Cheese. Salt to taste.

Serve right away, or transfer to a lidded container and refrigerate up to 1 week.

```
**********************
1 cup drained Creamy
  Kefir Cheese (page
  137)
1/4 cup Pickle Kraut
  (page 47), chopped
Kosher salt
**********************
```

Pickley Creamy Kefir Cheese
ABOUT 1 CUP

In a small bowl, fold the pickle and dill into the Creamy Kefir Cheese.

Serve right away, or transfer to a lidded container and refrigerate up to 1 week.

```
**********************
1 cup drained Creamy
  Kefir Cheese (page
  137)
1 small Sour Dill
  (page 39) or store-
  bought pickle,
  finely diced
2 tablespoons fresh
  dill, stemmed and
  minced
Kosher salt
**********************
```

Wine-Washed Aged Cheese

MAKES 3 WHEELS

A lot of Fermenter cheeses are aged for several months. Lucky for you, this recipe takes about a month. We sped things up for you since, for most of the time, the cheese will take up a good deal of space in your refrigerator. And because refrigerators all behave a bit differently, even though most are kept to 35 to 40 degrees F, I've given you a lot of physical cues throughout the cheese-aging process.

This cheese is slightly trickier to make than the Creamy Kefir Cheese (page 137) or Cheese Sauce Situation (page 184), but I believe in you. You'll only run into problems if you don't tend to it, and even then, it's hard to botch. I've unearthed wheels of this cheese in the cooler, that I've forgotten about, covered in mold, and I didn't shed any tears. Simply scrape the mold off and carry on. That said, washing your wheels in wine (or something else , see note on page 144) wards off outer fungal growth and also adds depth of flavor and texture. You can also add herbs and/or spices (page 146) and enjoy them a bit younger.

There's a nice hazelnut flavor and creaminess to this semi-hard, sliceable cheese. It ends up almost caramelly on the exterior, and a bit more intense on the inside. You can certainly slap it onto sandwiches, but I think it's best to showcase on its own. Serve your wheels with crackers on a snack board and invite all your cheese-loving friends over.

CONTINUED

MAKE THE CHEESE BASE TAKES: FOUR DAYS OR MORE
Make the Kefir-Cultured Hazelnut Cheese Base.

> **NOTE:** A note about the yield: from 4⅓ to 4½ cups of Kefir-Cultured Hazelnut Cheese Base you only need 3⅓ cups for this recipe. Use the remaining cup or so to make a mini tub of the Creamy Kefir Cheese (page 137), or a very small additional aged wheel.

FLAVOR THE CHEESE TAKES: ABOUT FIVE MINUTES
In the bowl of a high-powered blender (page 29), add the Kefir-Cultured Hazelnut Cheese Base, Chickpea Miso, yeast, porcini powder, and salt, and blend starting at low and slowly increasing the speed to medium, for 4 to 5 minutes, or until smooth.

STRAIN THE CHEESE TAKES: ONE WEEK
Set a medium fine-mesh sieve over a medium bowl, and line the sieve with a double layer of cheesecloth. Transfer the cheese mixture to the sieve, and then cover the sieve and bowl with plastic wrap.

Transfer the sieve/bowl to the refrigerator, and drain for 1 week. If your sieve does not sit fairly high above the bowl, you might want to empty the bowl's whey into a jar, to save it, once or twice. You don't want the cheese to sit on the whey. You will end up with ½ cup or more of whey, which keeps for roughly 2 to 3 months. Save it and use it, page 132. By the end of the week you should have about 2½ cups of the drained and thickened cheese mix.

FORM THE WHEELS TAKES: ABOUT FIVE MINUTES
Using a 3-inch-wide and 1½-inch-deep ring mold, dipped in water and set over a piece of two-ply cheese paper (place the cheese on the waxy side, not the shiny/polyethylene side), pack the cheese. With a spoon or spatula, transfer the cheese mix to the ring mold, pressing down on it to eliminate air bubbles. Smooth the top of the cheese.

Gently slide the mold off. Using your fingers or a wet spatula, lightly smooth the sides and top of the cheese. Repeat all of the steps above and shape two more wheels.

SALT & AGE TAKES: ABOUT TWO WEEKS
Lightly dust the tops of the wheels evenly with an ⅛ teaspoon of salt, divided. Transfer the wheels (on cheese paper) onto a wire rack or a bamboo sushi mat.

Put the rack or sushi mat over a rimmed baking sheet, and transfer it uncovered to your refrigerator. Air-dry for 4 to 5 days.

****
3¹/₃ cups Kefir-
   Cultured Hazelnut
   Cheese Base (page
   133)
¹/₃ cup Chickpea Miso
   (page 61) or a
   light/young store-
   bought miso
¹/₃ cup nutritional
   yeast flakes
1³/₄ teaspoon porcini
   powder (break up the
   dried porcini by
   hand and blend/food
   process/grind it
   into a powder)
³/₄ teaspoon fine sea
   salt, plus more for
   aging
¹/₄ cup white wine
   for wine-washing
   (optional, see
   note), something
   that you drink,
   that you have open,
   that's not too
   precious
****

CONTINUED

1   Flavor your cheese base.

2   Strain it over a large bowl.

3   Form wheels in your cheese molds on cheese paper.

4   Flip the cheese wheels after curing.

5   Wine-wash them with a pastry brush.

6   Wrap in clean cheese paper to ripen further.

Once the wheels are dry enough that you can flip them, carefully pick each one up and flip it onto fresh cheese paper. If they are still too wet, let them go another day or two. Use a spatula to smooth the tops and sides once flipped. Repeat this flipping plus salting (⅛ teaspoon of salt divided) every other day for 1 week. On no-salt days simply let the wheels air-dry and be.

> **NOTE:** For washing the cheese wheels, you do not have to use white wine. You can also use kraut or pickle brine, beer, cider, kombucha—whatever wash you want that's sweet or salty or a bit of both.

WINE-WASH TAKES: ABOUT ONE WEEK

Once the rind has developed, the wheels are easy to pick up, and there are most likely some fissures on the surface, start washing the wheels. Pour ¼ cup of white wine into a small-lidded container. With a pastry brush, brush the entire exposed surface. Try to smooth the fissures with the wine. Store the wine in the fridge for your next washing session.

For 4 days, with clean or gloved hands, flip and then wine-wash the portions of exposed cheese.

After day 4, stop washing the cheese. Let it continue to dry and develop its rind for 2 more days, flipping it once, until the exterior is almost waxy.

WRAP & RIPEN TAKES: AT LEAST ONE WEEK

Whenever your wheels look ready, remove them from the refrigerator, wrap them in cheese paper, and ripen them for 1 week.

Enjoy! I like our aged cheese best at room temperature. Store and refrigerate it in cheese paper for up to 1 month. Check the cheese and cheese paper every week or so. If it is funky or the cheese paper has gotten a bit wet, discard it and wrap in new paper.

AGED CHEESE CHEAT SHEET

NOTE: This is a very rough time frame. Please keep in mind that some of the steps below will take a day or two more than we have here, or a day or two less, depending on your conditions and your ingredients.

DAY 1 THROUGH 3 Make Kefir-Cultured Hazelnut Cheese Base (page 133).

DAY 3 THROUGH 10 Add ingredients (miso, porcini, salt, etc.) and strain cheese mix in a cheesecloth-lined sieve in the refrigerator.

DAY 10 After draining, form the cheese wheels with ring mold, salt the tops, and place on cheese paper on top of a rack or mat.

DAY 10 THROUGH 15 Store wheels uncovered in refrigerator.

DAY 15 Once dry enough to flip, carefully flip the wheels onto fresh cheese paper and salt the tops. Add herb- or spice-encrust (page 146) if you like and enjoy right away, or continue to age.

DAY 15 THROUGH 21 Flip and salt the wheels every other day; continue to store uncovered in refrigerator.

DAY 21 THROUGH 25 Flip and wash exposed portions of wheels daily.

DAY 25 THROUGH 27 Store wheels uncovered in refrigerator and flip once.

DAY 28 THROUGH 34 Wrap each wheel individually in cheese paper and refrigerate for at least 1 week before enjoying.

Herb-or-Spice-Encrusted Aged Cheese

****

ONE BRIN D'AMOUR WHEEL

1 teaspoon dried
  rosemary
1 teaspoon dried thyme
1 teaspoon dried
  oregano
1 teaspoon ground
  paprika
1 teaspoon whole
  coriander seeds

ONE BERBERE WHEEL

1 tablespoon ground
  berbere (Ethiopian
  spice blend)

**ONE FRESH & HERBY
WHEEL**

1 tablespoon minced
  fresh chives
1 tablespoon stemmed
  and minced fresh
  thyme
1 tablespoon stemmed
  and minced flat-leaf
  parsley

****

MAKES 3 WHEELS

For this recipe, simply follow all the Wine-Washed Aged Cheese (page 141) steps until you first flip them.

At this point, carefully roll them in whatever herb/spice mix you want. I've given you some suggestions at left, but please feel free to play around with what you have and like.

I recommend using 1 to 3 tablespoons of fresh or dried herbs or spices per wheel. In general, about 1 to 2 tablespoons of a dried spice mix and up to 3 tablespoons of a fresh herb mix work great. Maybe do a different herb and spice mix for each wheel? I like fines herbes, so equal parts fresh chives, tarragon, parsley, and chervil is lovely. Fresh dill is great too.

Either way, place your herbs or spices in a shallow bowl and gently roll and turn the wheels into it, pressing down slightly, until they are entirely covered. At this point, you can enjoy the wheels soft and young, or you can carry on aging and salting and flipping them as you do with the Wine-Washed Aged Cheese on page 144 after you've flipped them, just omit the wine-washing steps.

It's up to you. You have three wheels, so maybe enjoy one on the fresher side rolled in fresh herbs, another spiced one after an additional week or so of aging, and the third spiced after one more week of aging. Just be sure not to wine-wash the herb/spice-encrusted ones. I would be sad if you washed all your tasty herbs and spices away.

1   Once the wheels are dry enough that you can flip them (step 3 in Salt & Age), it's time to roll them in your herbs/spices.

2   Put your herbs/spice in a small, shallow bowl and gently roll and turn your wheels in them, one by one, pressing down slightly, until they are entirely covered.

3   At this point, enjoy the wheels soft and young, or carry on aging and salting them as you do with the Wine-Washed Aged Cheese on page 144 after you've flipped them, just omit the wine-washing steps.

NOTE: I like our aged cheese best at room temperature. Store and refrigerate it in cheese paper for up to 1 month. Check the cheese paper every week or so. If it is funky or the cheese paper has gotten a bit wet, discard it and wrap in new paper.

When Did Vegan Cheese Suddenly Become Good?

My earliest memories of eating vegan cheese are from when I first
became vegetarian in sixth grade. I went to the local health food
store and got myself some Soya Kaas cheese. It had a windmill on the
label and looked like a legit good thing. It was not. It was the worst
block of fucking horribleness I've ever eaten. I don't know if they
still make it, but I sure fucking hope not. It should be outlawed.

There was a change, somewhere along the line, when people like
Miyoko Schinner of Miyoko's Creamery, and others like her, got
into it. When Miyoko's first book came out—*Artisan Vegan Cheese*—
people's perceptions about what vegan cheeses were and could be
dramatically shifted.

For a long time, there was this goal for vegan cheese to simply be
an analog of real cheese. When you abandon that notion—I mean it never
will be—and start making a thing that you're proud of on its own, with
its own unique characteristics (hello, water kefir as cheese culture!)
that's when you can really do something special.

People still make analogs, and I'll admit that those have also
improved greatly. There are companies like Violife and others that use
food science to engineer vegan ingredients into cheese-like stuff. I'm
not as interested in that as I am in craft vegan cheese. People like
the vegan cheese wizard Karen McAthy of Blue Heron Creamery in Canada
delve a bit into food science, but are way more rooted in the craft
perspective as are we. Want to wash our hazelnut aged cheese in sour
pickle brine? Heck yeah, go for it!

When we first started making cheeses at Fermenter, we didn't even
use the word "cheese" because we wanted to make something that wasn't
all about evoking dairy cheese. I think that pushing expectations when
you're making craft vegan cheese—so not trying to emulate Swiss, Brie,
or whatever—is best.

So come up with your own names and don't dash people's expectations.
If you call it Swiss, well guess what, people will want it to be like
Swiss cheese—duh—and whatever that means to them. If it's a vegan
product, it simply will never ever be like that. Free your vegan
cheese! Let it be its own thing.

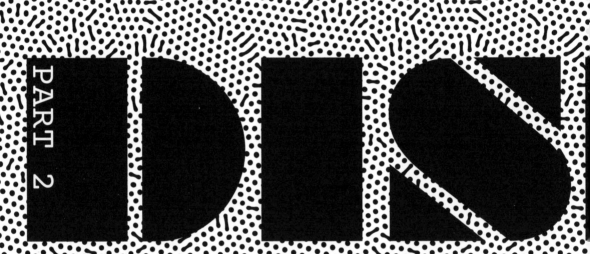

PART 2

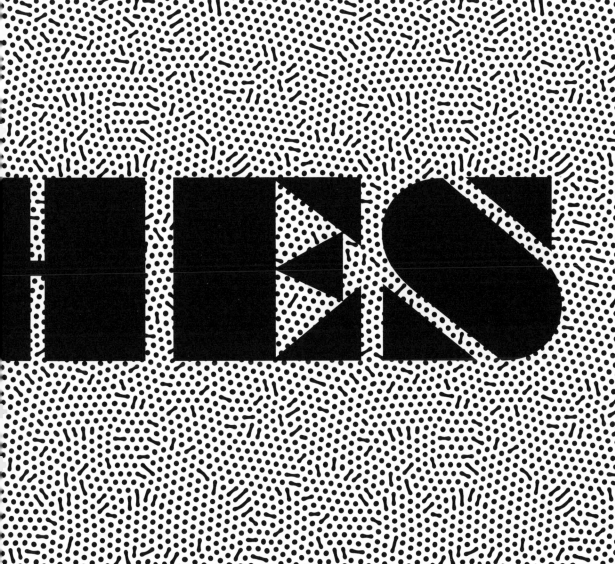

So You Made Some Tasty Ferments. Now What Do You Do with Them?

As a youngin who really enjoyed Doc Martens and anything Ben Sherman, I loathed all things hippie. I'm talking Birkenstocks, crystals, mud-soaked music festivals, thoughtless cultural appropriation, annoying platitudes on peaceful living, not washing with soap . . . OK, apparently, I still have my issues with hippies. But gosh darn I've adopted a great deal of hippie culture throughout the years, including ditching meat from my diet and trading in my boots and braces for comfy clothes.

And let's not forget about hippie food! It can be really, really tasty, and it's usually healthy and thoughtfully local and organic. The problem is largely one of aesthetics and tone for me, as I'm never going to call something on my menu a Buddha Bowl (there's that thoughtless cultural appropriation again!), and I never want a menu of mine to read in gratitudes. I'm saying this with the full knowledge that some "patriot" with a 12-foot American flag streaming behind his lifted 4x4 would quickly call me a hippie. I'm not mad about it—it's all relative. I'd rather be a smelly hippie any day of the week than a fascist.

So how do we take all those great hippie-food techniques and ingredients and incorporate them into a more digestible aesthetic? In other words, how do we meet the challenge of making our so-called fancy hippie food, you ask? We do it by taking all those delicious and nutritious hippie ingredients—a lot of them ferments from Part 1 of this here book-and putting them into familiar forms—burgers, sandwiches, salads, bowls, etc. We use the highest-quality ingredients and a lot of techniques that we learned over our collective years in fine dining. Most importantly, we don't take ourselves too seriously, as hippies are often wont to do.

Listen, at the end of the day all are welcome (except fascists) at Fermenter, as long as you laugh at my bad jokes.

FANCY, PLANT-BASED HIPPIE FOOD

BLET

(a.k.a. Tempeh Bacon + Lettuce + Shio Koji–Glazed Eggplant + Tomato on Sourdough)

MAKES 4 SANDWICHES

Can you get more savory than *shio koji*–glazed eggplant with thick ripe slices of tomatoes and homemade tempeh bacon? Nope! The first time I had koji and eggplant together was in an eggplant *misozuke* at Nobu in Tribeca in the early 2000s. They cured eggplant in miso and then charcoal grilled it. I'd never experienced flavors like that before.

Try to make this sandwich with juicy summer tomatoes that are super ripe and perfect. A big heirloom variety with sweet acidity and not too many seeds is best. If you have crummy tomatoes, don't bother. And, start making your Tempeh Bacon about a week before making these.

1   With a knife, lightly score the flesh on both sides of each eggplant slice with 3 to 4 diagonal crisscross cuts. Salt each slice with ½ teaspoon of salt evenly divided between both sides.

2   Transfer the salted eggplant slices to a colander in your sink or over a bowl, and weigh them down with a heavy plate or bowl for about 30 minutes.

3   After 30 minutes, rinse the salted eggplant with water in order to remove the salt. Slather each slice with 1½ tablespoons of Shio Koji. Put the eggplant in a container large enough to fit it all, cover, and refrigerate for at least 3 and up to 4 hours.

4   When you're ready to cook the eggplant, shake off any excess Shio Koji—save it, you can reuse it (page 70)! In a large pan over medium heat, heat 2 tablespoons of the oil. Fry the eggplant, flipping it occasionally, for 6 to 8 minutes, until it is nicely charred, soft, and collapsing. Remove the eggplant to a paper towel–lined plate and set it aside.

5   Wipe off the pan and over medium-low heat, heat the remaining 3 tablespoons of oil. Fry the Tempeh Bacon, flipping it occasionally, for 5 to 7 minutes, until it's golden brown and cooked through. Remove the tempeh bacon to another paper towel–lined plate.

6   Lightly toast the bread, and slather each slice with 1 tablespoon of Miso Sauce.

7   Build yer sandwich! Arrange two slices of lettuce on the bottom half of the bread, then layer each with three to four slices of Tempeh Bacon, two tomato slices, and finally, two slices of eggplant. Top with the remaining slices of bread. Slice each sandwich down the middle and serve.

****
1 to 1½ pound
  eggplant, sliced
  into 8 (½-inch-
  thick) rounds
1 tablespoon plus 1
  teaspoon kosher salt
¾ cup Shio Koji (page
  70) or store-bought
  shio koji
¼ cup plus 1
  tablespoon sunflower
  oil or other neutral
  oil, divided
¾ pound Tempeh Bacon
  (page 88) or store-
  bought tempeh bacon,
  sliced into 12 to
  16 (¼-inch-thick)
  slices
8 slices sourdough
  bread
½ cup Miso Sauce
  (page 161), or 7
  tablespoons Aquafaba
  Mayo (page 201)
  or store-bought
  vegan mayo with
  1 tablespoon of a
  light/young store-
  bought miso whisked
  in
8 slices red leaf or
  butter lettuce
8 thick slices ripe
  tomato (from about 2
  medium tomatoes)
****

CONTINUED

Koji Beet Reuben

MAKES 4 SANDWICHES

Every vegetarian or vegan place that I've ever worked at has had a tempeh Reuben on the menu, and I think that's just great. Truly. When we were creating Fermenter, we didn't want to stray too far from the traditions of the prototypical vegetarian/vegan restaurant, but we did want to do things a bit differently. So . . . meet our Koji Beet Reuben. Savory, satisfying, and also beautiful with its deep-hued slices of koji'd ruby beet. This sandwich is the closest thing we have to a proper deli sandwich. It's one of my favorites.

For a little background, we got really inspired by the beet charcuterie they were doing over at Jeremy Umansky's Larder Delicatessen & Bakery in Cleveland. A few years ago, I took Rich Shih's class on koji. With Jeremy, Rich co-authored the book we read cover to cover and love dearly: *Koji Alchemy: Rediscovering the Magic of Mold-Based Fermentation*. Soon after that class, we started making a version of their beet charcuterie.

Right away it was like, "Heck yes, let's get this into production!" I tuned up the Ruby Kraut to fit the sandwich a bit better, and we already had the Miso Sauce, which I simply reworked into our Horseradish Special Sauce with a bit of horseradish and ketchup. The Chive Creamy Kefir Cheese was a perfect fit, and we landed a good rye. There you have it. Just be sure that you start by making the Koji Beets (and the Ruby Kraut and Chive Creamy Kefir Cheese) about a week before you want to whip these up.

1 In a large pan over medium heat (no oil!), cook the Koji Beets, flipping them a couple times, for 3 to 4 minutes, or until warmed through. Add the Ruby Kraut, mix them together, and cook for 1 to 2 minutes more, until the kraut is warmed through. Season the mixture to taste.

2 Lightly toast four slices of the rye, spread 3 tablespoons of Chive Creamy Kefir Cheese on each slice, and top with the beet-kraut mixture, dividing it equally among the slices.

3 Lightly toast the remaining four slices of rye. Spoon 2 tablespoons of Horseradish Special Sauce on each. Top the sandwiches with the sauced slices.

CONTINUED

```
**********************
2 pounds Koji Beets
  (page 73), sliced
  into 1/8- to 1/4-inch-
  thick slices
1 1/3 cups Ruby Kraut
  (page 51)
Kosher salt and freshly
  ground pepper
8 slices deli rye
3/4 cup Chive Creamy
  Kefir Cheese (page
  138)
1/2 cup Horseradish
  Special Sauce (page
  160)
2 tablespoons sunflower
  oil, other neutral
  oil, or vegan
  butter, divided
**********************
```

4   In a large pan over medium heat, heat 1 tablespoon of the oil or butter. Place two sandwiches in the pan and cook for 2 to 3 minutes, until the bread is a nice golden brown. Carefully flip them and cook for 2 to 3 more minutes.

5   Transfer the sandwiches to a paper towel–lined plate. Add the remaining tablespoon of oil or butter to the pan and repeat with the other two sandwiches.

6   Slice the Reubens in half diagonally—careful, the beets slip around a good deal—and stick a couple of those frilly toothpicks in the sandwich halves if you've got them.

Horseradish Special Sauce

MAKES 1 CUP

You know you're going to love this one. I mean, would you just look at how simple it is? Everyone likes a special sauce, and this one has its own added kick from the fermented horseradish, miso, and smoked paprika. I'm thinking it might just be your new favorite condiment.

```
**********************
2 tablespoons Fermented
   Horseradish (page
   161) or 1 tablespoon
   of store-bought
   horseradish
3/4 cup plus 2
   tablespoons Miso
   Sauce (page 161), or
   3/4 cup Aquafaba Mayo
   (page 201) or store-
   bought vegan mayo
   with 2 tablespoons
   Chickpea Miso (page
   61) or a light/young
   store-bought miso
   whisked in
2 tablespoons Tomato
   Ketchup (page 162)
   or store-bought
   ketchup
1 teaspoon smoked
   paprika
**********************
```

1   In a small bowl, combine the Fermented Horseradish, Miso Sauce, Tomato Ketchup, and smoked paprika, and stir to combine.

2   Store in the refrigerator for up to 2 weeks.

Fermented Horseradish

MAKES ½ CUP

If you can find fresh horseradish root, fermenting your own horseradish is super easy and way better and cheaper than store-bought. Don't stress, though, if you can't source any fresh horseradish. Our recipes that call for it work just fine with store-bought.

1 Pack the horseradish into a half-pint or smaller jar and add the water to cover it. Either tare/weigh your horseradish and water to determine the amount of salt to add (page 7), or simply add a ½ teaspoon. Stir to combine.

2 Wipe down the headspace of your jar, place a piece of plastic wrap on the top of the horseradish (right on it), cover the top of the jar with a lightweight, breathable cloth, and secure it with twine or a rubber band.

3 Store the horseradish at room temperature (55 to 75 degrees F) and out of direct sunlight for 5 to 7 days, until it's tangy and to your taste. It keeps, refrigerated, for up to 2 months.

```
**********************
3- to 4-inch piece
   (about 2 ounces)
   fresh horseradish
   root, peeled and
   finely grated
1/4 cup plus 1
   tablespoon water
2 percent fine sea
   salt by weight, or
   1/2 teaspoon
**********************
```

Miso Sauce

MAKES ABOUT 1 PINT

Our crazy-good Miso Sauce is a flavorful mayo replacement, and it's super tasty in our Fermenter Bowl (page 187) and as a dipping sauce for whatever you've got: sliced veggies, bread, your finger. If you want to make a salad dressing out of it, simply add some minced cornichons and fines herbes, or a bit of lemon zest and basil.

1 In a blender, combine the Chickpea Miso, water, garlic, nutritional yeast, and salt. Puree on medium to high speed for about 1 minute, or until smooth.

2 With the machine still running, add the oil in a slow, steady stream to emulsify. This should take about 1 minute. Once the sauce is thick and emulsified, stop the machine and taste it. Season with more salt if necessary.

3 Store the sauce in the refrigerator for up to 1 week. Every couple days, burp it (see Burp Your Babies, page 10) and give it a stir.

```
**********************
3/4 cup Chickpea Miso
   (page 61) or a
   light/young store-
   bought miso
1/2 cup plus 2
   tablespoons water
1 clove garlic, minced
1/2 teaspoon
   nutritional yeast
   flakes
Pinch kosher salt
3/4 cup sunflower oil
   or other neutral oil

**********************
```

CONTINUED

Tomato Ketchup

MAKES ABOUT 1 PINT

****
$^1/_2$ cup red wine
   vinegar
$^1/_2$ cup organic pure
   cane sugar
$^1/_4$ teaspoon fine sea
   salt
1 star anise
1 allspice berry
1 clove
1 bay leaf
$^1/_4$ teaspoon black
   peppercorns
2 cups tomato puree
****

Ketchup has a really interesting history if you want to geek out on it. It came to Europe in the 1600s from China's Fujian Province, and originally it was a pickled fish brine or sauce. The closest thing to it these days is probably Malaysian *kecap manis*—a thick, savory, soy-based sauce. In the nineteenth century, there were recipes for all different types of ketchup: mushroom ketchup, walnut ketchup, etc. Essentially, you took those ingredients, along with vinegar and sugar, and then pureed, strained, and seasoned it. It's really fun to push this recipe in different flavor directions too—roasted red pepper ketchup, curry ketchup. I love both of those and encourage you to experiment.

For the spice sachet here, I recommend using a bit of cheesecloth tied together at the top with kitchen twine, but use whatever you have on hand and like to properly contain the spices.

1   In a small pot over medium heat, add the vinegar, sugar, salt, and spice sachet filled with the star anise, allspice, clove, bay leaf, and peppercorns. Bring the mixture to a boil, then reduce the heat and simmer for 15 to 20 minutes, or until the mixture is slightly syrupy and lightly coats a spoon.

2   Add the tomato puree, and simmer, stirring occasionally, for another 10 to 15 minutes, or until it thickens to a pasta-sauce consistency. Be careful when you stir it, it can spit! Set the ketchup aside to cool to room temperature, then remove and discard the spice sachet.

3   In a blender or the bowl of a food processor, add the ketchup and puree on medium to high speed for 20 to 30 seconds, or until smooth. Pass it through a fine-mesh sieve to get it to the smooth consistency of a proper ketchup. Season with additional salt to taste. Store the ketchup in the refrigerator for up to 3 months.

Almost Famous Fermenter Burger

MAKES 5 BURGERS

My biggest complaint with veggie burgers, most of which are grain- and bean-based, is that they fall apart. Almost every time! I wanted a solid piece of tempeh for our burger, but it took some time to figure out how to make the patty chewy, sturdy, and moist, while at the same time super savory and delicious.

Our secret weapon, which does all that and then some, is our Smoked Onion Shio Koji. It breaks down the tempeh proteins, adds deep umami, and also gives the patty a killer sear. You can shortcut the marinade by using our straight-up Shio Koji (page 70) or a store-bought one as the marinade. And you can use store-bought veggie burgers instead of making the patties. Marinate and cook the store-bought burgers the same way we do our from-scratch patties. They won't be as tasty, but they'll still be really freaking good. Just know that our tempeh patties take 2 to 3 days to make, so plan accordingly if you want to make them for this burger that is *almost* famous. To make every recipe that goes into this burger, see Top-to-Bottom Fementer Burger (page 166).

1   Using clean or gloved hands, carefully dip the Tempeh Burger Patties into the Smoked Onion Shio Koji. Put the patties on a plate and marinate them for at least 1 hour before cooking them or up to 2 days, refrigerated. (You can also freeze them up to 3 months; four burgers fit side by side in a 1-gallon zip-top freezer bag. Place them flat in the freezer.)

2   In a medium or large pan (depending on how many burgers you are cooking), heat 1 tablespoon of oil per burger patty over medium heat. Once the pan and oil are hot, after about 1 to 2 minutes, shake off any excess marinade and store or discard. Add the patties to the pan. Cook for 3 to 4 minutes on each side, or until they have a nice char and some serious browning.

CONTINUED

****

$^1/_2$ recipe Tempeh Burger Patties (page 91) or 5 store-bought tempeh or veggie burger patties

$1^1/_4$ cups Smoked Onion Shio Koji (page 71) or store-bought shio koji

5 tablespoons neutral oil, plus more for toasting buns

5 burger buns, halved and toasted

$^3/_4$ cup Miso Sauce (page 161) or $^1/_2$ cup plus 2 tablespoons Aquafaba Mayo (page 201) or store-bought vegan mayo with 2 tablespoons of a light/young store-bought miso whisked in

$^1/_3$ cup Tomato Ketchup (page 162) or store-bought ketchup

5 to 15 leaves red leaf lettuce

5 slices tomato, sliced crosswise

5 thin slices sweet onion

5 Sour Dills (page 39) or store-bought pickles, sliced crosswise

****

NOTE: You can cook these patties on a griddle, but I would stay away from baking or grilling them—they just won't be as good without that yummy oil-in-pan-browning.

3   Once your patties are cooked, hooray! The sun's suddenly out; now get those burger buns out! Add oil and toast them (page 166). To build the burgers, spread the buns with 1 heaping tablespoon Miso Sauce on each half. Add about 1 tablespoon Tomato Ketchup to the top bun. Place 1 to 3 pieces of lettuce on each bottom bun, then a patty. Top with a slice of tomato, 1 slice of onion, and 4 or 5 slices of Sour Dills.

NOTE: Cook frozen patties (no need to defrost them first) for 5 to 6 minutes per side. You might need a teaspoon more of oil per frozen patty, depending.

Top-to-Bottom Fermenter Burger

Take your burger game to the next level by making each and every recipe that goes into our Almost Famous Fermenter Burger and then throw a killer burger party. Invite me!

TOASTED TOP BUN
For our burgers, we use Portland's Dos Hermanos Bakery vegan hamburger buns. They're yummy, chewy burger buns with a good amount of flavor. I really do love a softer bun for our burger too—like a store-bought potato or sesame seed bun. Whatever bun or buns you use, halve them and brush them with a neutral oil. In a medium or large pan over medium heat, toast the buns cut side down for 1 to 2 minutes, or until nicely toasted.

SOUR DILLS (PAGE 39)
Follow our Sour Dills & Pickle Brine recipe, or use some quality store-bought pickles. Thinly slice one of these Sour Dills into pickle chips for each burge-one whole Sour Dill per burger. Place them right in the Miso Sauce and Tomato Ketchup on the top toasted bun. Go ahead and put a whole pickle or two on the side of each burger too. You deserve it.

MISO SAUCE (PAGE 161)
Slather 1 heaping tablespoon on the top bun.

TOMATO KETCHUP (PAGE 162)
Add roughly 1 tablespoon of Tomato Ketchup onto the top bun along with the Miso Sauce.

SLICE OF SWEET ONION LIKE VIDALIA OR WALLA WALLA

SLICE OF TOMATO IF IT'S SUMMER
If it's not summer, they're a bummer.

TEMPEH BURGER PATTIES (PAGE 91), PAN-SEARED

A PIECE (OR TWO OR THREE) OF RED LEAF LETTUCE

MORE MISO SAUCE
Slather 1 heaping tablespoon on the bottom bun.

TOASTED BOTTOM BUN

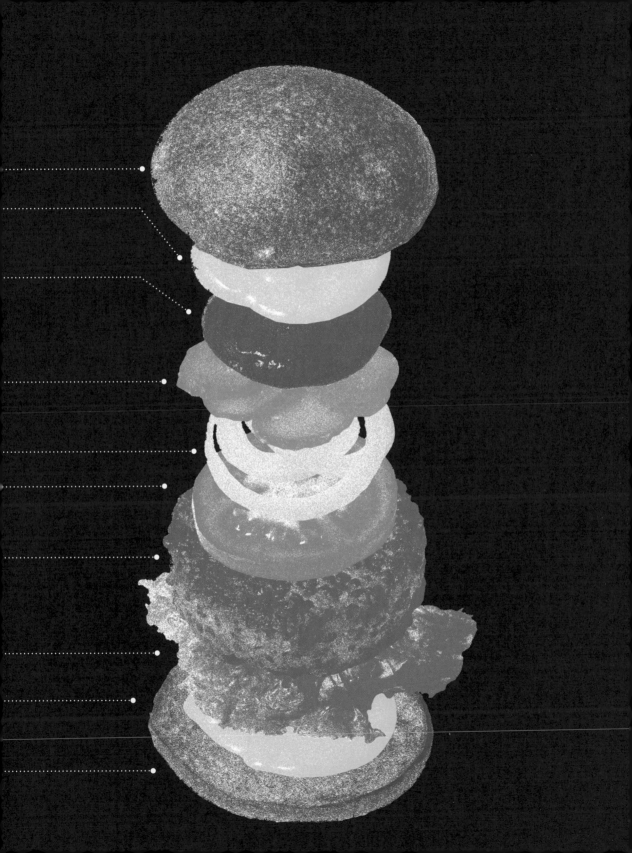

BBQ Tempeh Sammy

with Poppy Seed Slaw & Coffee BBQ Sauce

MAKES 4 SANDWICHES

This is a hearty, over-the-top summer sandwich that reminds me a lot of my time living in Jacksonville, Florida, before I was vegan. While I lived there, I went to a lot of really good barbecue spots, and I'd almost always get slices of white bread with barbecue and mop sauce. So that's the old glory—the food nostalgia—we were chasing for this one.

The slaw here was also inspired by Jacksonville, where I had slaw dogs for the first and only time in my life. Have you had them before? It's pretty simple. They take coleslaw and pile it high onto hot dogs. There you have it. I've never had them anywhere else, and they're so dang good. Even more than the sum of their parts. There were two types of hot dogs in Jacksonville that I never had anywhere else: slaw dogs and splitters. For splitters, you simply fry the dogs in a deep fryer so they split and curl up. We're not doing that at Fermenter. Yet.

Don't forget to start making your Pinto Bean Tempeh several days before you want to make these sammies. Or you can use store-bought tempeh.

1   In a small bowl, stir together the Shio Koji and ½ cup of the Coffee BBQ Sauce.

2   In a container large enough to fit the Pinto Bean Tempeh slab, slather both sides of it with this marinade, cover, and refrigerate overnight (12 or more hours).

3   The next day, shake off any excess marinade and store for future use or discard. In a large pan over medium heat, heat 2 tablespoons of the oil. Fry the tempeh slab whole, flipping it occasionally and brushing it a few times with the remaining ¼ cup of Coffee BBQ Sauce, for 6 to 8 minutes, or until it is nicely browned on both sides.

4   Transfer the tempeh to a cutting board to cool. Once it's cool enough to handle, cut it into 12 to 16 slices and set them aside.

CONTINUED

```
*********************
2 tablespoons Shio
  Koji (page 70) or
  store-bought shio
  koji
3/4 cup Coffee BBQ
  Sauce (page 171) or
  store-bought BBQ
  sauce, divided
1 (1-pound) slab Pinto
  Bean Tempeh (page
  85) or store-bought
  tempeh
3 tablespoons plus 1
  teaspoon sunflower
  oil or other neutral
  oil, divided
8 slices soft sourdough
  sandwich bread or
  white bread
1 cup Miso Sauce (page
  161), or 3/4 cup
  plus 1 tablespoon
  Aquafaba Mayo (page
  201) or store-bought
  vegan mayo with 3
  tablespoons Chickpea
  Miso (page 61) or a
  light/young store-
  bought miso whisked
  in
2 cups Poppy Seed Slaw
  (page 170)
5 or 6 Sour Dills (page
  39) or store-bought
  pickles, thinly
  sliced lengthwise
*********************
```

5 Brush one side of each slice of bread with ½ teaspoon of the remaining oil. In a large pan over medium heat, toast the bread, oiled side down, for 3 to 4 minutes, or until its nicely browned. You'll probably need to do this in two to three batches.

6 Spread each slice with 2 tablespoons of Miso Sauce on the non-toasted side. Layer half of the bread with three to four slices of the seared tempeh, ½ cup of the Poppy Seed Slaw, and finally, four or five Sour Dill pickle slices. Top with the remaining four slices of Miso Sauce–dressed bread, toasted side up. Slice each sandwich down the middle and serve.

Poppy Seed Slaw

MAKES ABOUT 1 QUART

I always love poppy seeds in slaw. They're the first thing I think of when I think of slaw. I think that BBQ and coleslaw are just naturally good friends—reminiscent of picnics and summertime. I love how slaw adds its bright, crunchy, tasty vibe to our savory, hot, barbecued tempeh, which reads almost like tempeh ribs in this sandwich.

1 In a small pan over medium-low heat, heat the oil. Add the green garlic and cook, stirring regularly, for 5 to 6 minutes, or until it is fairly wilted. Remove the pan from the heat and set it aside to cool.

2 In a large bowl, combine the cooled green garlic, cabbage, carrots, Aquafaba Mayo, cilantro, olive oil, Apply Cider Vinegar, poppy seeds, and salt. Store the slaw in the refrigerator for up to 3 days.

****
2 teaspoons sunflower oil or other neutral oil

¹/₂ cup thinly sliced green garlic, or ¹/₂ cup thinly sliced scallions plus 2 cloves garlic, thinly sliced

4 cups thinly sliced green cabbage (from ¹/₂ small head)

1 cup peeled and grated carrots (from 2 medium carrots)

¹/₂ cup Aquafaba Mayo (page 201) or store-bought vegan mayo

¹/₄ cup chopped fresh cilantro leaves

2 tablespoons extra-virgin olive oil

2 tablespoons Apple Cider Vinegar (page 100) or store-bought cider vinegar

1¹/₂ teaspoons poppy seeds

¹/₄ to ¹/₂ teaspoon kosher salt
****

Coffee BBQ Sauce

MAKES ABOUT 1 QUART

This sauce is so dang good, and I just know you're going to love it. Make this sandwich, and after that use this sauce for all of your barbecue needs. It's great on tofu, tempeh, all the veggies, etc.

For the spice sachet here, I recommend using a bit of cheesecloth tied together at the top with kitchen twine, but use whatever you have on hand and like to properly contain the spices.

CARAMELIZE THE ONIONS TAKES: ABOUT 30 MINUTES

In a medium pan, heat the oil over medium-low heat. Add the onion, garlic, and salt, and cook for about 30 minutes, stirring occasionally and being careful not to burn the onions, until they're deep golden brown and caramelized.

Add the coffee to the pan to deglaze it and scrape up any bits with a spatula. Increase the heat to medium, and simmer the sauce for 5 minutes, or until it reduces by about a quarter. Set it aside.

SOAK THE CHIPOTLES TAKES: AT LEAST 20 MINUTES

In a medium bowl, cover the chipotles in the boiling-hot water and soak them for at least 20 minutes while you prepare the gastrique.

MAKE THE GASTRIQUE TAKES: ABOUT 30 MINUTES

In a small pot over medium heat, bring the Apple Cider Vinegar, sugar, and spice sachet filled with the anise seeds, allspice berries, peppercorns, and cinnamon stick to a boil. Reduce the heat and simmer for 25 to 30 minutes, or until the gastrique is slightly syrupy, lightly coats a spoon, and is reduced by about half. Set it aside.

MAKE THE SAUCE BASE TAKES: ABOUT 10 MINUTES

In a blender add the caramelized onions, chipotles with their soaking liquid, gastrique, tomato puree, molasses, sugar, and ground spices, and puree on low speed, gradually increasing the speed to high, for 5 to 6 minutes, or until the sauce is smooth.

SIMMER TAKES: ABOUT 40 MINUTES

Pour the sauce into a medium heavy-bottomed pot over high heat and bring to boil. Once the sauce is boiling, reduce the heat to medium-low. Then simmer, stirring occasionally, for 30 to 40 minutes, until it's nice and thick.

CONTINUED

****
FOR THE CARAMELIZED ONIONS

1 tablespoon sunflower oil or other neutral oil
3 cups thinly sliced yellow onion (from about 1¼ medium yellow onion)
1 clove garlic, minced
½ teaspoon kosher salt
2 cups freshly brewed coffee

FOR THE SOAKED CHIPOTLES

3 dried chipotles, stemmed
½ cup boiling-hot water
****

INGREDIENTS CONTINUED ⟶

****

FOR THE GASTRIQUE

1¹/₂ cups Apple Cider
   Vinegar (page 100)
   or store-bought
   cider vinegar

1 cup organic pure
   cane sugar

¹/₂ teaspoon anise
   seeds

3 allspice berries

3 black peppercorns

1 small cinnamon stick

FOR THE SAUCE BASE

3 cups tomato puree
   (from a 28-ounce
   can)

¹/₄ cup blackstrap
   molasses

2 tablespoons organic
   pure cane sugar

¹/₄ teaspoon freshly
   (and finely) ground
   black pepper

¹/₄ teaspoon ground
   allspice

¹/₄ teaspoon paprika

¹/₄ teaspoon garlic
   powder

¹/₈ teaspoon ground
   ginger

¹/₈ teaspoon anise
   seeds, finely ground

¹/₈ teaspoon ground
   cinnamon

****

SMOKE THE SAUCE TAKES: ABOUT 1 HOUR

If you don't have a smoker or simply don't want to unearth it for this sauce, I recommend adding 1 scant to heaping (depending on your taste) tablespoon of liquid smoke at this point and then carrying on with passing the sauce through the fine-mesh sieve. The BBQ sauce won't be as good, but it'll still be pretty dang tasty.

Prepare a smoker. If it has a temperature gauge, set it to the lowest temperature possible.

Transfer the sauce to a shallow, heatproof dish (a pie pan works great for this), and place it in your preheated smoker. Smoke with applewood or another fruitwood for about 1 hour.

Remove the sauce from the smoker and let it cool. Once it's cool enough to handle, strain it through a fine-mesh sieve, using a ladle to push it through, into a medium bowl.

Store the sauce in a lidded container in the refrigerator for up to 3 months.

"He's a Survivor"

I don't know if you ever saw the 2000 movie *The Way of the Gun*, but James Caan plays Joe Sarno, an old, grizzled fixer for a mobster. At some point Sarno is talking to these two young professional security guys and says, "You want to know the only thing you can assume about a broken-down old man? It's that he's a survivor." I always really liked that. The idea that in life you have to roll with the punches and keep on rocking.

I had the idea ingrained in me from a young age that in order to prove myself I had to be hard. I had to deal with pain, just say "Fuck it," and be hardcore. That kind of mindset is definitely what the kids these days call toxic masculinity. 100 percent. I was always trying to be that guy.

Here's a kitchen example. At Portobello, my first restaurant in Portland, where I was chef-owner from 2009 to 2013, we'd have this contest of how long you could hold your arm in ice water. We would fill a 24-quart tub full of ice water and we'd all put our arms in it. Pretty quickly, after a couple minutes, people started peeling out right and left. And I thought, after everyone was done and gone, Fuck yes, I won! But even that wasn't enough. I had to really show them. I held my stupid arm in there for 24 minutes. Yep.

It was utterly and completely painful, it totally sucked, and I didn't care. I had to prove to everybody that I could deal with more pain and more bullshit than any of them. I can take it all, and I will take it all. Keep giving me more and more pain, and more and more shit, and I'll take all of it. I'll even make something good of it. That was so, so important to me to prove to people. Shovel whatever the fuck you want on me, and I absolutely will not go down. Ever.

Unfortunately, what that sort of twisted survival instinct turned into after many years was a diagnosed anxiety disorder. My brain started kicking in and basically made me think I was dying. All the time. I had so many panic attacks. I would go into work with tunnel vision, a rapid heartbeat, and an overwhelming sense of dread. Fun! The irony is that I had less stress and less things to worry about at that time overall. I actually manufactured anxiety for myself. It still lingers, and I can easily get overwhelmed. Suffice it to say, these days I'm way more comfortable in my garden than a crowded bar.

What's the lesson here? Don't go for the toxic masculinity crap. And don't endlessly compare yourself to other people. We all deserve respect for who we are. Trying to be something for other people can really fuck with you. It made me a real asshole, for sure, and it made everyone I worked with completely miserable for many years. Try to relax, please: it's just food.

Pinto Bratwurst Hoagie

with Giardiniera & Kombucha Mustard

MAKES 4 DOGS

This is another one of those meaty classics that we wanted to re-create as plant-based at Fermenter. Whether you grew up eating something like this at the ballpark or at summer barbecues, sausage hoagies are nostalgic. The spice blend in our bratwurst is traditional and delicious. We actually had a German customer come through in 2022 and say that our dressed bratwurst was the most German thing, vegan or not, that he tasted while visiting the States. *Abklatschen!,* a.k.a. a high-five in German.

We often serve our sausage as detailed here, but you can also sub griddled onions or any of our krauts (pages 45–51) for the giardiniera and feel great about it.

1   Lightly toast your hoagie buns and spread 2 tablespoons of Miso Sauce and 1 tablespoon of Kombucha Mustard on each.

2   In a large pan over medium heat, heat the oil. Carefully add the sausages to the pan, turning them every 2 to 3 minutes so that they get nice and browned. Cook for 5 to 8 minutes, or until the sausage's interior registers 165 degrees F on a meat thermometer, covering for the last minute or so of cooking.

3   Place a sausage in each bun and top each sausage with ½ cup of Spicy Giardiniera. Serve and eat immediately, as the sausages deflate a bit as they cool.

NOTE: These sausages also steam up nicely, although I prefer them crisped a bit and browned in the pan. If you steam them, increase the cook time to 10 to 12 minutes and flip them once about halfway through. If cooking from frozen, steam for 12 to 15 minutes.

CONTINUED

****
4 hoagie buns
$^1/_2$ cup Miso Sauce
  (page 161), or 7
  tablespoons Aquafaba
  Mayo (page 201)
  or store-bought
  vegan mayo with
  1 tablespoon of a
  light/young store-
  bought miso whisked
  in
$^1/_4$ cup Kombucha
  Mustard (page 179)
  or store-bought
  whole grain mustard
2 tablespoons plus 2
  teaspoons sunflower
  oil or other neutral
  oil
4 Smoked Pinto
  Bratwursts (page
  176; see note)
2 cups Spicy
  Giardiniera (page
  53) or store-bought
  giardiniera
****

```
***********************
Applewood or another
    fruitwood, for
    smoking
2 (1-pound) slabs
    Pinto Bean Tempeh
    (page 85) or store-
    bought tempeh
3/4 teaspoon yellow
    mustard seeds
1/2 teaspoon coriander
    seeds
1/2 teaspoon caraway
    seeds
11/4 teaspoons freshly
    ground black pepper
3/4 teaspoon ground
    nutmeg
3/4 teaspoon dried
    oregano
1/2 teaspoon ground
    ginger
3/4 teaspoon onion
    powder
1 cup plus 2
    tablespoons ice-
    cold water (see
    note), plus more for
    smoking the tempeh
3 tablespoons
    methylcellulose HV
    (page 18)
3/4 cup sunflower oil
    or other neutral oil
2 tablespoons kosher
    salt
1/4 cup plus 2
    tablespoons
    nutritional yeast
    flakes
***********************
```

Smoked Pinto Bratwursts

MAKES 8 TO 10 SAUSAGES (ABOUT 5 CUPS OF SAUSAGE FILLING)

There was a lot of trial and error involved in landing on the right texture for our pinto bratwursts. It turns out that while the proportions of the ingredients are really important, the execution and method are equally as important.

The methylcellulose HV that this recipe calls for is used to thicken and stabilize the sausage; otherwise it'll be too soft and squishy. When methylcellulose HV is heated, it creates a firm and elastic gel that mimics meat fat, so the sausage actually plumps up. Be sure to serve these sausages hot because methylcellulose HV is thermoreversible, meaning that when it cools and chills, it will be soft again—almost gooey. It's not good, so please don't use this for sausages that you want to enjoy chilled.

In terms of flavor, our bratwurst has that complexly spiced black peppery bite enhanced by nutmeg, oregano, ginger, and onion powder that all great bratwurst—whether meaty with pork and veal or vegan—should have. One bite and it will transport you to the German beer hall of your dreams—a vegan one!

NOTE: When you hydrate the methylcellulose HV, be sure that you do so with ice-cold water. Either put your water in the fridge overnight before making the recipe or make ice water and strain it.

SMOKE THE TEMPEH TAKES: 1 TO 1½ HOURS

Prepare your smoker. If it has a temperature gauge, set it to the lowest temperature possible. You don't want to cook the tempeh at all at this stage, just smoke it.

Place the Pinto Bean Tempeh slabs in your preheated smoker with a pan of water set underneath them on the bottom. Smoke the tempeh for 1 to 1½ hours, depending on if you prefer a moderately smoky flavor to a quite smoky flavor, with applewood or another fruitwood. The longer you smoke it, the smokier it gets, obviously.

Remove the tempeh from the smoker and let it cool to room temperature.

TOAST & GRIND THE SPICES TAKES: 2 TO 4 MINUTES

Toast the mustard seeds, coriander seeds, and caraway seeds (see Toast Your Spices, page 12), and then combine them, once cooled, with the pepper, nutmeg, oregano, ground ginger, and onion powder. Blend the spice mix in a coffee grinder for 30 seconds or so, until finely ground.

MAKE THE METHYLCELLULOSE GEL TAKES: 40 MINUTES OR MORE

Add the ice-cold water to a high-powered blender. Start blending at medium speed. With the blender running, add the methylcellulose HV. Increase to high speed and blend for about 10 seconds, until it is very thick and the motor starts to struggle. Refrigerate the lidded blender bowl with the methylcellulose gel for 30 minutes or more.

MAKE THE SAUSAGE MIXTURE TAKES: AN HOUR OR MORE

Dice the smoked tempeh into roughly ¼-inch dice (it might completely fall apart when you do this, and that is A-OK), and transfer it to a medium bowl. Add the oil, salt, nutritional yeast, and ground spice mix and blend well. Refrigerate for 30 minutes or more.

> **NOTE:** At this point, before you've added the methylcellulose gel, the sausage mix makes a great hash. Simply pan-fry it. You don't even need to add any oil because it's already in the mix.

Remove the chilled smoked tempeh and methylcellulose mix from the refrigerator. Fold the methylcellulose mix into the tempeh. It will be very thick and sticky, almost like melted marshmallows. You won't be able to get all of it out of the blender. Don't worry: get what you can.

> **NOTE:** If your blender has a self-cleaning function, use it. Whipped methylcellulose is super-duper sticky and takes some time to clean out.

Fully mix the sausage and methylcellulose with a large wooden spoon, while being careful to retain a good amount of methylcellulose strands. In other words, don't overmix the sausage, thereby negating methyl's cool binding properties. Also, don't undermix it and end up with big blobs of methyl gel. Ewwwww. Refrigerate the sausage mix for 20 minutes or more.

CONTINUED

FORM THE BRATWURST TAKES: ABOUT 10 MINUTES

Top a baking sheet with parchment paper. With clean hands, shape the tempeh mix into classic-shaped sausages, using a ½ cup to a heaping ½ cup per sausage. The former will give you about 10 sausages, the latter about eight. The sausage mix is quite oily, so you don't need to wet your hands to shape it. You can also use plastic wrap to help roll and form them.

Alternatively, you can stuff the mix into vegan sausage casings with a sausage machine like we do, twisting the casings to link them, or, shape them into patties if you want. Cover the sausages and refrigerate them for up to 2 days.

> **FREEZING & COOKING BRATWURST FROM FROZEN:** The shaped sausages freeze surprisingly well. Shape and wrap each individually in plastic wrap, and then freeze them in a freezer bag for up to 3 months. Be sure to shape them before freezing, since once frozen, you don't want to mess around with the sausage mix much or you'll weaken the methylcellulose strands.
>
> When cooking from frozen, don't defrost them: simply add 2 to 3 minutes to the overall cook time. And if you pan-fry them, put the lid on the pan for the last 2 to 3 minutes of cook time.

Kombucha Mustard

MAKES ABOUT 1 QUART

I got my love of mustard from my half-Prussian dad. While I was growing up, he was always eating some sort of powerful grainy mustard with his smoked braunschweiger or liverwurst. He literally takes coarse mustard, mixes it with frozen veggies, and then microwaves them. He loves it.

Because of my dad, I gravitate toward coarse mustard. Our Kombucha Mustard gives you the best of both worlds since you blend half of the mustard seeds and leave the rest whole. It's really important here to soak and drain your seeds twice for at least 12 hours, so budget at least a day before you can enjoy the mustard. It might seem like a step you can shorten or maybe even skip, but don't bother making our mustard without giving your seeds the full and proper soaking that they and you deserve. If you don't, you'll end up with something that's more of a weapon than a food.

****
$1/2$ cup plus 1
  tablespoon brown
  mustard seeds
$1/2$ cup plus 1
  tablespoon yellow
  mustard seeds
$1/4$ cup white wine
  vinegar
$1/4$ cup Kombucha Honey
  (page 180) or store-
  bought vegan honey
2 tablespoons Botanical
  Kombucha (page 107)
  or store-bought
  floral/botanical
  kombucha
1 teaspoon kosher salt
****

1   In a medium bowl, add the brown and yellow mustard seeds, and cover them in water by a few inches. Soak them overnight (12 hours or more).

2   The next day, in a fine-mesh strainer, drain and rinse the mustard seeds. Put the mustard seeds back in the bowl, and cover them again in water by a few inches. Soak them overnight (12 hours or more) for a second time.

3   Drain and rinse the mustard seeds again. Transfer them to a large mixing bowl. Whisk in the vinegar, Kombucha Honey, and Botanical Kombucha, until the honey is incorporated.

4   In a high-powered blender (page 29), add roughly half of the mustard mix. Blend for 4 to 5 minutes, or until fairly smooth. Return the smooth mustard to the mixing bowl. Add the salt and stir to incorporate the whole seeds into the smooth mustard. Wait at least 1 day before serving. Store the mustard in an airtight container in the refrigerator for up to 3 months.

CONTINUED

Kombucha Honey

MAKES ABOUT 1 PINT

****

1 quart apple juice,
  preferably from
  your local farmers'
  market
2 cups Botanical
  Kombucha (page 107)
  or store-bought
  floral/botanical
  kombucha
³/₄ cup freshly
  squeezed lemon juice
  (from about 3 medium
  lemons)
2 cups organic pure
  cane sugar
2 tablespoons dried
  rose hips, in a
  sachet

****

We were inspired to make our own honey because we'd tried some commercial vegan versions, and although they were decent, we wanted to get at our own super-special honey flavor and texture. We're also always looking for more places to use our kombucha. Since the Botanical Kombucha already has such a honeyed flavor from all of the botanicals, we had a hunch it might be a good addition. It is!

This honey goes into our Kombucha Mustard for sweetness and texture, but it's good in and on so many different things. My favorite: stir it into our Sunflower Yogurt (page 130), and then drizzle it over a yogurt bowl with whatever fruits and granola-type crumbly things you've got. Oh, and please don't substitute another juice for the apple juice here because its pectin, sugars, and color all work their magic.

1 In a medium pot over high heat, add all the ingredients and bring to a boil, stirring initially to dissolve the sugar. Reduce the heat to low, then simmer for about 2½ hours, or until the honey is thick and syrupy, coats a spoon, and has reduced to roughly 2 cups.

2 Remove the pan from the heat, discard the sachet, and let the honey cool. When it has cooled, pour the honey into a glass jar or lidded container. Store it in the refrigerator for up to 3 months.

Cheesy Jojo Supreme
with Tempeh Bacon

MAKES 4 SERVINGS

When I was a kid, I was obsessed with stuffed potato skins. Lucky for me, in the '80s they were one of the most popular restaurant appetizers in mall cafés on the West Coast—with roasted elephant garlic hot on their heels. At the Stanford Mall in Pleasanton, California, one town over from where I grew up, there was a café serving them. Chubby little Aaron couldn't get enough.

Since you really don't see them in restaurants anymore, I decided to come up with something like them. It turns out that these are really more like jojo nachos, but whatever. Optional step: get really stoned before gorging for maximum effect.

1   Preheat the oven to 400 degrees F and line a baking sheet with parchment paper.

2   In a medium bowl, toss the potato wedges to coat with the Koji Seasoning Salt and oil.

3   Transfer the potatoes to the prepared baking sheet and bake, flipping once about halfway through, for 30 to 35 minutes, or until golden and crispy.

4   On a large plate or platter, pile the baked jojos. Pour the warmed Cheese Sauce Situation over them first, followed by the Sour Cream–Like Situation. Top them with the Pickled Red Onions, Tempeh Bacon, and cilantro. Either drizzle everything with the Hot Behind Hot Sauce, or serve it on the side for dipping.

NOTE: Follow the steps on page 157 for pan-frying the Tempeh Bacon, using 2 to 3 teaspoons of sunflower oil for frying.

CONTINUED

****

2 medium russet potatoes (1 to 1¼ pounds), each sliced into 6 to 8 wedges (jojos)

½ cup Koji Seasoning Salt (page 184)

¼ cup sunflower oil or other neutral oil

¾ to 1 cup Cheese Sauce Situation (page 184), warmed

3 to 4 tablespoons Sour Cream-Like Situation (page 185)

2 to 3 tablespoons chopped Pickled Red Onions (page 198)

2 to 4 ounces Tempeh Bacon (page 88) or Smoke Pinto Bratwurst (page 176) or store-bought vegan bacon or sausage, chopped and pan-fried (see note)

1 to 2 tablespoons chopped fresh cilantro leaves

2 to 4 tablespoons Hot Behind Hot Sauce (page 41) or our Spicy Sauce (page 193) or store-bought hot sauce

****

Koji Seasoning Salt

MAKES 1 PINT

****
1¹/₂ cups Koji Rice
    (page 63)
20 bay leaves
1 tablespoon plus
    1 teaspoon dried
    oregano
³/₄ cup plus 2
    tablespoons gluten-
    free all-purpose
    flour (we prefer
    Bob's Red Mill)
3 tablespoons kosher
    salt
1 tablespoon smoked
    paprika
1 tablespoon onion
    powder
1 tablespoon piment
    d'Espelette
****

This seasoning salt is the magic behind our Cheesy Jojo Supreme, but it's also super tasty as a tempeh or tofu seasoning, and I love it on breakfast potatoes. Pull out your dehydrator for this one because you'll need it to properly dry your Koji Rice. You definitely want to cook with this and not just sprinkle it on things as is, because of the flour. If you *do* want to sprinkle it on and not cook something—popcorn, chip dip, etc.—simply omit the flour. How about that for a work-around?

1   Set a dehydrator to 95 degrees F, or to the dehydrator's lowest setting. Place the koji rice in a wide dish or pan and dehydrate for 3 or more hours.

2   Using a food processor or a large coffee grinder, grind the dehydrated rice to a fine powder. You should end up with ¾ cup plus 2 tablespoons.

3   Using a coffee grinder, grind the bay leaves and oregano into a fine powder.

4   Combine all the ingredients in a medium bowl. Store the salt in a jar at room temperature for up to 6 months.

Cheese Sauce Situation

MAKES 1 PINT

****
¹/₄ cup sunflower oil
    or other neutral oil
1 medium yellow onion,
    sliced
1 clove garlic, minced
³/₄ teaspoon smoked
    paprika
¹/₂ teaspoon piment
    d'Espelette
¹/₄ teaspoon cumin
    seeds
1 cup water, divided,
    plus more for
    blending
1 cup Creamy Kefir
    Cheese (page 137)
2 tablespoons
    nutritional yeast
    flakes
³/₄ teaspoon kosher
    salt
****

This sauce is great on our Cheesy Jojo Supreme, of course, but give it a shot on our burger (page 163) or use it as a nacho topper or anywhere else you'd normally put melty, yummy cheese. Think of it as the type of cheese you'd pump out of a dispenser at 7-Eleven if they somehow magically became vegan. You get it. Oh, and be sure to start your Creamy Kefir Cheese at least a week before you plan to make this. It takes that long to make and there isn't a great substitution for it here.

1   In a medium pan over low heat, heat the sunflower oil. Add the onion and garlic and cook for 4 to 5 minutes, or until the onion has released some of its liquid.

2   Add the paprika, piment d'Espelette, and cumin seeds, and cook for about 3 more minutes, or until they are smelling super-duper. Add ¾ cup of the water. Increase the heat to medium-high and bring the onion mixture to a boil. Boil for about 5 minutes, stirring regularly.

3   Transfer the mixture to a high-powered blender. Add the remaining ¼ cup of water, Creamy Kefir Cheese, nutritional yeast, and salt.

4   Blend the sauce, starting at low speed and slowly increasing to medium speed, for 5 to 7 minutes, or until completely smooth. If the engine struggles, add 1 tablespoon of water at a time up to 3 tablespoons so that the blade can move continuously.

5   Enjoy the *situation* right away or keep it warm in a double boiler (a heatproof bowl set over a pot filled with 2 to 3 inches of simmering water). Or let it cool and store it in the refrigerator for up to 2 weeks. It thickens when it cools. Reheat it gently over low heat, stirring regularly.

Sour Cream–Like Situation

MAKES 1 CUP

We like to dress up our Sunflower Yogurt for our Cheesy Jojo Supreme, but you can also use it straight up and it'll be delicious. It's looser than sour cream, really more like a crema.

In a blender, process all the ingredients for about 1 minute, or until smooth. Store in the refrigerator for up to 2 weeks.

> **NOTE:** If you use store-bought yogurt, this Sour Cream–Like Situation will be significantly thinner because our yogurt is thicker than most commercial ones, so I'd recommend using just ¼ cup of water.

****
¾ cup Sunflower Yogurt (page 130) or store-bought vegan yogurt

½ teaspoon lactic acid powder (we use Druids Grove vegan lactic acid) or citric acid

½ cup water (see note)

1½ teaspoons sunflower oil or other neutral oil

½ teaspoon kosher salt
****

The Fermenter Bowl

MAKES 4 LARGE BOWLS

What we were aiming for with this megabowl was a nice combo of accessible, filling, nutritious, and affordable deliciousness. Nailed it. This is one of our most popular dishes at Fermenter, and it's a really fun one to prep at home. Make all of the components over the weekend—note that the beans need to soak for 12 or more hours, so plan accordingly—and then enjoy our bowl for lunches and/or dinners throughout the week. My wife, Jenny, does that for us pretty regularly—what a sweetheart (see Sunshine Cookies, page 205).

Jenny and I recently got some really big bowls—I'm talking more than quart-size—to serve these and other things in at home. So yeah, get out the big bowls, the MONSTER bowls! And if you really want to show your vegan colors, top your Fermenter Bowl with, oh, I don't know, a few cups of nutritional yeast. Then you're a certified, card-carrying vegan.

1   Get whatever large bowl or bowls you want and put the Herby Quinoa on the bottom as your base. Top the quinoa with the Braised Beans, Seasonal Savory Roasted Vegetables, Kale Salad, and sauerkraut, mounding them around the bowl kind of like Korean bibimbap. It'll all get mixed together and eaten up, but to start, keep everything in the bowl separate, like a colorful, edible vegan mosaic.

2   Then drizzle the whole shebang with 2 tablespoons (or more! I like mine seriously saucy) of whichever sauce you want—you can obviously combine sauces too. That's it. Serve and enjoy. Oh, and if you're feeling extra hungry, how about some pan-fried Pinto Bean Tempeh (page 85) on top? Yeah, go ahead and do that.

CONTINUED

```
*********************

AMOUNTS PER LARGE
BOWL:
1 cup Herby Quinoa
  (page 188)
1 cup Braised Beans
  (page 189), warmed
1/2 cup Seasonal Savory
  Roasted Vegetables
  (page 191), warmed
1/2 cup Kale Salad
  (page 192)
1/4 cup sauerkraut of
  your choosing, such
  as North Coast Kraut
  (page 45)
2 tablespoons Miso
  Sauce (page 161),
  Yogurt Sauce (page
  193), or Spicy Sauce
  (page 193)

*********************
```

Herby Quinoa

MAKES ABOUT 1 QUART

****

1 cup dry organic
  quinoa
1/4 preserved lemon
  (rind and flesh),
  rinsed well, seeded,
  and finely minced,
  or the finely grated
  zest plus juice of
  1/2 lemon
2 tablespoons minced
  fresh flat-leaf
  parsley leaves
2 tablespoons minced
  fresh chives
2 tablespoons minced
  fresh dill leaves
2 tablespoons extra-
  virgin olive oil
1/4 to 1/2 teaspoon
  kosher salt

****

When I became vegan, it was a prerequisite to like quinoa. Then somewhere along the way, I learned that quinoa is pretty horrible for the Andean people who cultivate it. It's overextracted from the region for hippies and so-called socially conscious people in the Northern Hemisphere, making it unavailable for the growers because of the overextraction and resulting price inflation. Fucking hell.

For a long time I was like, "No quinoa for me, thanks." And then I found out Kevin Schurter was growing it up here: Willamette Valley Quinoa. Perfect! Now we can enjoy delicious quinoa and not be scumbags. Kevin is a full-time fireman and a part-time farmer. He bred ornamental quinoa with edible varieties in order to develop his hardy quinoa. So cool.

This salad is all about fresh green herbs and Kevin's delicious quinoa. There's nothing else to it other than preserved lemon, a little salt, and a lot of love. Oh, and we cook quinoa at Fermenter a little differently than most. We cook it more like pasta, so there's no sad, soggy, bottom-of-the-pot quinoa.

1   Fill a large-lidded pot three-quarters full with lightly salted water and bring to a boil over high heat.

2   Meanwhile, line a baking sheet with a piece of muslin or a clean, lightweight, lint-free towel. In a fine-mesh sieve, rinse the quinoa for about 30 seconds, or until the water runs clear. This is a very important step. Quinoa is covered in saponin, and if you don't rinse all of it off, your quinoa will be bitter.

3   Add the rinsed quinoa to the pot, and put the lid on it until it returns to a boil. Once it's boiling, remove the lid and cook for 8 to 12 minutes, or until it's fully done. Strain the quinoa in a fine-mesh strainer and transfer it to the prepared baking sheet, spreading it evenly. Fluff it with a fork to let steam out and let it cool to room temperature.

4   Once the quinoa is cool, transfer it to a medium bowl. I find that gathering up the towel, carefully opening it over the bowl, and then brushing the quinoa off by hand works well. Add the lemon, parsley, chives, dill, and olive oil. Stir well to incorporate and season with salt to taste. Store the quinoa in the refrigerator for up to 1 week.

Braised Beans

MAKES ABOUT 1 QUART

These braised beans are super savory and produce a really rich pot likker (a.k.a. bean water). They soak for 12 or more hours, so they end up really tender and bloated, and that's important—no firm individual beans, please! It makes me mad when I see that. It's OK for a bean salad, I guess, but not for braised beans. And if you pull beans out of the pot, blend them, and add them back to the pot to make them nice and thick, well, I think you're cheating. Remember, I have all-seeing eyes (page 128)! Please don't do that. I'm not pushy about much anymore these days, but I am pushy about braised beans.

Please note that the quarter onion, quarter bell pepper, garlic cloves, and dried *guajillo* chilies that the beans soak with, and then initially cook with, all go in whole, as opposed to the minced versions of the first three that go in later for the second simmer. You can leave those whole veggies, garlic, and chilies in at the end, like my *abuelita* and I do (they're pretty broken up by that point anyway), or you can pull them out. Also, as my *abuelita* always says, "If more guests are coming, throw more water on the beans." Great advice.

DAY ONE

In a medium pot that you'll cook the beans in the next day, add the beans, onion, bell pepper, garlic, bay leaves, and *guajillo* chilies, and cover with the water. Soak at room temperature overnight (12 or more hours).

> NOTE: The next day, don't pour out the soaking water! It's very important that your soaking water is also your bean-cooking water. Trust me.

DAY TWO

Transfer the pot to the stove and bring everything to a boil over high heat, then lower the heat and simmer the mixture for about 1 hour, until the veggies and beans are soft and the bean water has begun to thicken. Skim off and discard any foam as the beans cook. If at any point the pot gets dry, simply add a ½ cup of water at a time.

While the beans simmer, in a medium pan over medium-low heat, heat the olive oil. Add the onion, bell pepper, garlic, and cumin. Cook, stirring occasionally, for 12 to 15 minutes, or until the onions are translucent. Add this to the pot of beans, along with the salt, and stir to combine.

CONTINUED

```
*********************
DAY ONE
1¹/₂ cups dried rojo
    chiquito beans or
    other small red or
    black beans, picked
    over, rinsed, and
    drained
¹/₄ yellow onion,
    peeled
¹/₄ green bell pepper,
    seeded
3 cloves garlic,
    peeled
2 to 4 bay leaves
2 dried guajillo
    chilies, stemmed
7 cups water
DAY TWO
3 tablespoons extra-
    virgin olive oil
¹/₂ yellow onion,
    minced
¹/₂ green bell pepper,
    seeded and minced
2 cloves garlic,
    minced
1 tablespoon ground
    cumin
1 scant to heaping
    tablespoon kosher
    salt
*********************
```

My Mother

My mother, Linamelia, was born in Pinar del Río, Cuba, and came to the States in 1960 as a young girl. She grew up in a fairly tight-knit family and community in the East Bay. When I was growing up, my mom mostly cooked adventurously and mostly not Cuban food, but it was her classic Cuban dishes that always seemed so special to me.

Let's talk my mom's black beans, why don't we? Time after time I'm disappointed by so-called Cuban black beans at restaurants. They are often too sweet, wrongly spiced, thin, or undercooked. You need the right ingredients, including the beloved and humble cachucha pepper, to make proper Cuban black beans. This is why, despite my heritage, I don't serve black beans at Fermenter. We can't consistently get cachuchas locally, so I won't dishonor my mother's beans by putting them on the menu. Hers will always be better, regardless. I'll just keep on making other beans.

My mother, of course, taught me a lot more than just how to cook beans.

The biggest lesson she taught me: "It's better to ask for forgiveness than for permission." This has been especially excellent advice when it comes to navigating the bureaucracies of city and county government as a small-business owner, that's for sure. It's been a supporting philosophy in my fuck-shit-up, DIY ethic for many years.

I love my mother dearly and wouldn't be here writing this book if it weren't for her. I mean, duh, she gave birth to me. Her support throughout the years has been immeasurable. She's picked me up every time I've fallen down.

Return the beans to high heat, bring to a boil, and then lower the heat and simmer for about 30 minutes, or until the beans are fully cooked. At this point the bean water should be thickened, sort of like a gravy. You want the beans to pour from the ladle, but not be so loose that they're soupy.

Remove and discard the bay leaves (and the quartered yellow onion, bell pepper, and *guajillo* chilies if you like), and serve the beans immediately, or let them cool to room temperature and store them in the refrigerator for up to 1 week. But don't reheat the beans more than once because they will become too mushy and too thick and lose flavor.

Seasonal Savory Roasted Vegetables
MAKES ABOUT 1 QUART

Roast some seasonal vegetables, yo! They're delicious and will make your home smell good and feel cozy. Just keep an eye on them so that they get to that perfectly browned, roasty-toasty state. Heartier and denser veggies will take closer to 50 minutes and juicier and softer veggies will take closer to 20.

In the spring and summer, you might try a mix of summer squash, sweet onion, and mild peppers. And in the fall/winter maybe a mix of Brussels sprouts, carrots, and parsnips? Roast whatever you want, but those are a couple tasty combos.

You'll want to use about 6 cups of veggies if you're roasting something dense, such as potatoes or carrots, and about 8 cups if you're roasting high-moisture veggies such as eggplant or onions.

```
***********************
6 to 8 cups chopped
  vegetables cut into
  1- to 3-inch pieces
3 to 4 tablespoons
  extra-virgin olive
  oil, depending
  on the amount of
  veggies you're
  roasting
1/2 to 1 teaspoon
  kosher salt
1/4 to 1/2 teaspoon
  freshly ground black
  pepper
***********************
```

1 Preheat the oven to 425 degrees F.

2 In a medium bowl, add the veggies and olive oil, and toss to coat. Season with the salt and pepper, and stir to combine.

3 Transfer the veggies to a baking sheet, spreading them evenly in a single layer, and roast for 20 to 50 minutes, or until they are tender and lightly browned.

4 About halfway through the roasting time, remove the pan from the oven and flip the vegetables. Serve them right away, or let them cool to room temperature and store them in the refrigerator for up to 1 week.

CONTINUED

Kale Salad

MAKES ABOUT 1 QUART

```
***********************
1 bunch (1/2 pound)
    green kale
1/4 cup plus 2
    tablespoons Kale
    Dressing (see below)
***********************
```

Hello, straight-up massaged kale salad! Does that sound good to you? (Exactly how hippie are you?) This salad is basically thinly sliced green kale massaged with the dressing. Easy! You can add a cup or so of sauerkraut to this if you want to add a little zing. If you've never rolled up your kale to chiffonade it, I bet you'll enjoy doing that here. It's fun.

1   Stem the kale either by hand or with a knife. Stack several of the leaves at a time and roll them up tightly from base to top. Once tightly rolled, slice the roll crosswise into ¼- to ½-inch-wide slices. And then chop into 1- to 3-inch pieces.

2   In a large bowl, massage the kale with the Kale Dressing with clean hands for about 2 minutes. Eat it right away, or store it in the refrigerator for 1 day.

Kale Dressing

MAKES 1 PINT

```
***********************
Juice of 2 medium
    lemons (about 1/2
    cup)
1 clove garlic, minced
1 cup Aquafaba Mayo
    (page 201) or
    store-bought vegan
    mayonnaise
1/2 cup nutritional
    yeast flakes
1/2 cup extra-virgin
    olive oil
1/4 to 1/2 teaspoon
    kosher salt
***********************
```

This is a really handy little sauce to have around. Beyond the salad, it's great on rice, and I also like to toss it with steamed veggies. The inspiration was simple: every single vegan hippie household that I've ever been to or lived in always layers their kale salad with tons and tons of nutritional yeast and good fats. Fermenter is basically a vegan hippie household occupied by a bunch of old punks with attitude.

1   In a blender or the bowl of a food processor, add the lemon juice, garlic, Aquafaba Mayo, and nutritional yeast, and blend on medium-to-high speed for about 30 seconds, or until smooth.

2   With the machine still running, add the oil in a slow, steady stream to emulsify it; this should take about 1 minute. Season with the salt. Chill the dressing until you're ready to use it. Store it in the refrigerator for up to 2 weeks.

Yogurt Sauce

MAKES 1 PINT

This tasty sauce is simply our Sunflower Yogurt dressed up with added fat and seasonings. It's nice and light with a zippy, garlicky, sunflower-y tang.

1 In a blender or the bowl of a food processor, combine the Sunflower Yogurt, oil, garlic, nutritional yeast, and salt. Process on medium to high speed for 1 to 2 minutes, or until smooth. Store the sauce in the refrigerator for up to 2 weeks.

   NOTE: If you use store-bought yogurt, your sauce will be significantly thinner because our yogurt is thicker than most commercial ones. It'll still taste delicious.

****

$1^1/_4$ cups Sunflower Yogurt (page 130) or store-bought vegan yogurt (see note)

$^1/_2$ cup plus 2 tablespoons sunflower oil or other neutral oil

2 cloves garlic, minced

$1^1/_4$ teaspoons nutritional yeast flakes

$^1/_2$ to $^3/_4$ teaspoon kosher salt

****

Spicy Sauce

MAKES 1 PINT

In addition to the Fermenter Bowl, our lemony Spicy Sauce is great with grilled summer squash and charred carrots, on tacos and quesadillas, and on our Cheesy Jojo Supreme (page 183). It's also a killer burger topper. So easy and so good.

1 In a medium pan over medium-low heat, heat the oil. Add the onion, chilies, and green garlic. Cook, stirring occasionally, for 12 to 15 minutes, or until the onions are translucent. Transfer the onion mix to a plate or small baking sheet and refrigerate until chilled.

2 Transfer the chilled onion mix to a blender. Add the lemon zest and juice, and blend for 1 to 2 minutes, or until fairly smooth. Add the cilantro, parsley, and salt and blend for 1 to 2 more minutes, or until the sauce is very smooth and well blended. Chill before serving. Store the sauce in the refrigerator for up to 1 week.

****

$^1/_4$ cup sunflower oil or other neutral oil

1 medium yellow onion, sliced

6 fresh Sarit Gat chili peppers or other small, spicy chilies, chopped

4 stalks green garlic, or 3 scallions plus 2 cloves garlic, sliced

Zest and juice of 4 medium lemons

1 cup chopped cilantro, stems and leaves

$^1/_2$ cup chopped flat-leaf parsley, stems and leaves

2 teaspoons kosher salt

****

I Just Want People to Feel Loved

The Cuban staple meal that I loved the most while growing up, and that I go back to over and over again—vegan version or not—is picadillo (Cuban ground beef hash with lots of garlic, onions, olives, and raisins), with black beans and rice (Moros y Cristianos) and either tostones or *maduros* and mojo. Give me all that on a plate and I'm one happy dude. I make all those dishes when I'm feeling nostalgic, and it always feels good to share.

The most memorable time I made a proper Cuban family style meal was the last time I saw my grandfather, Ramiro Sr., before he died. He was suffering from dementia and didn't recognize me. My mother, Linamelia, was taking care of him, and my wife, Jenny, was with me. What I most wanted for my grandpa at that point was a proper gathering of family—all of us sitting down together to enjoy a good home-cooked meal. I guess that deep down I was hoping if I set the scene, played the right music, and served up those familiar dishes, my grandpa would recognize me. About halfway through the meal, he turned to my mom and asked in Spanish, "Who are these people?"

I was a little heartbroken, but then I saw him really enjoying the meal, and that became enough. We were living in the moment, and I knew that during our dinner, my *abuelo* was happy. He was content. So mission accomplished.

That night, I made him picadillo (a vegan version), tostones and *maduros*, black beans and rice, and yuca frita—all the foods he liked. I made him empanadas and *ensalada de aguacate*. I put on music and played a song he loved called "Perfidia." He reminisced about Cuba that night and told us a few stories.

I think what makes me happiest when it comes to food—what I most want to do—is to make people feel loved. I believe that everyone deserves dignity, respect, and love, and to feel taken care of. The way I can give all that to people is with a lovingly prepared meal.

Boneless Broth

MAKES ABOUT 2 QUARTS

In eighteenth-century Paris, restaurants were places that served rich and restorative broths—the French verb *restaurer* means "to restore." By law they weren't allowed to serve anything beyond broth. Allegedly, in the mid-1700s when a restaurateur named Boulanger served sheep's feet in a white sauce, he was supposedly sued for not sticking to restorative broths and encroaching on another's business territory. Boulanger won the lawsuit and then, guess what? Restaurants began serving all different foods. Not just broths. So the story goes . . .

Whatever happened, I love sipping on yummy broths throughout the fall and winter. Fill a big thermos with our piping-hot Boneless Broth and drink it all day. It will keep you so warm and cozy. And added bonus: it's anti-inflammatory, thanks to the healthy dose of turmeric.

For me, it's best as a sipper in a mug, but you can certainly do other things with it. Throw in some sautéed vegetables and make a hearty soup. Add some ravioli or rice or noodles if you want.

1   In a small pot, add the onion, carrot, celery, ginger, garlic, bay leaves, and thyme. Add 2 tablespoons of the oil and stir to combine.

2   Put the pot over medium-low heat (lean more toward low than medium, because you want to gently sweat the veggies and herbs) and cook, stirring regularly, for 10 to 15 minutes, or until everything is fairly wilted and the veggies have released some juices at the bottom of the pot.

3   Add the turmeric, and cook, stirring regularly, for 2 to 3 minutes, or until the turmeric is fragrant. Deglaze the pan with 1 cup of the water, stir well, and transfer everything to a large pot.

4   Add the remaining 8½ cups water, the kombu, Lapsang souchong, and peppercorns to the pot, and stir to combine. Over high heat, bring to a full boil, then remove the pot from the heat and set it aside to steep for about 1 hour.

5   After an hour, strain the broth through a cheesecloth-lined fine-mesh sieve and whisk in the Chickpea Miso. Serve it right away. Stir in ⅛ teaspoon of olive oil per cup when serving, and be sure to give the broth a good stir before ladling it because the miso settles.

REFRIGERATING AND FREEZING THE BROTH: Cool the broth to room temperature and store it in the refrigerator for up to 1 week or in the freezer for up to 6 months. Defrost to room temperature and then reheat.

```
**********************
1 medium yellow onion,
  thinly sliced
1 medium carrot,
  peeled and thinly
  sliced
2 stalks celery,
  thinly sliced
1 (3- to 4-inch) piece
  of fresh ginger,
  unpeeled and thinly
  sliced
1 large head garlic,
  cloves peeled and
  chopped
2 bay leaves
3 to 4 sprigs thyme
2 tablespoons extra-
  virgin olive oil,
  plus 1 teaspoon for
  serving
1 tablespoon plus 1
  teaspoon ground
  turmeric
9¹/₂ cups water,
  divided
3 ounces dried kombu
1 tablespoon plus 1
  teaspoon Lapsang
  souchong tea leaves
1 teaspoon black
  peppercorns
¹/₂ cup Chickpea Miso
  (page 61) or a
  light/young store-
  bought miso
**********************
```

Hidden Willamette Valley Ranch Salad

MAKES 4 TO 6 SERVINGS

I love a big, loaded salad, and this one incorporates so many different tasty flavors and textures: our sweet and smoky Tempeh Bacon, toasted Oregon hazelnuts, our sweet and bright Pickled Red Onions, and, of course, our killer Sunflower Yogurt Ranch Dressing.

In the winter, we often add more shredded cabbage to it, while in the spring and summer, we favor lighter greens. The dressing, which is built from our Sunflower Yogurt (page 130), might also get a little lighter when the days are long. Be sure to make the Pickled Red Onions at least a day in advance of when you want to serve the salad. They're good the day of, but are tarter and more flavorful if you wait at least a day.

1   In a large pan over medium-high heat, toast the hazelnuts for 4 to 6 minutes, stirring or shaking the pan occasionally, until the nuts turn a darker brown and are fragrant and toasted. Remove the pan from the heat, and transfer the hazelnuts to a large plate or platter to cool. Once they're cool enough to handle, rub off the hazelnut skins as best you can (wrap the nuts in a towel and agitate them) and finely chop the hazelnuts. Set aside.

2   In a large pan over medium-low heat, heat the oil. Fry the Tempeh Bacon, flipping the cubes occasionally, for 4 to 5 minutes, or until they're golden brown and cooked through. Transfer the tempeh to a paper towel-lined plate.

3   In a large bowl, toss together half of the hazelnuts, and all of the cabbage, lettuce, carrots, Pickled Red Onions, parsley, chives, dill, and Sunflower Yogurt Ranch Dressing. Season with salt and black pepper to taste. Divide the salad evenly among plates or bowls. Top each evenly with the remaining hazelnuts and the Tempeh Bacon, and serve immediately.

CONTINUED

****

2 cups raw hazelnuts

1/4 cup sunflower oil or other neutral oil

1 pound Tempeh Bacon (page 88) or store-bought tempeh bacon, diced

1 1/4 pounds green cabbage (about 1 small head), thinly sliced into 1- to 2-inch pieces (8 cups total)

8 ounces red leaf lettuce (about 1 medium head), thinly sliced into in 1- to 2-inch pieces (8 cups total)

2 cups peeled, grated carrots (from about 4 medium carrots)

1 1/2 cups Pickled Red Onions (page 198), sliced into 1- to 2-inch pieces

1/4 cup chopped fresh flat-leaf parsley leaves

1/4 cup chopped fresh chives

1/4 cup chopped fresh dill leaves

2 cups Sunflower Yogurt Ranch Dressing (page 199)

Kosher salt and freshly ground black pepper

****

Pickled Red Onions

MAKES 1 QUART

****
2 medium red onions,
    thinly sliced
1 cup white wine
    vinegar
³/₄ cup organic pure
    cane sugar
¹/₄ cup plus 2
    tablespoons water
Pinch of kosher salt
****

Pickled red onions are a really popular restaurant pantry staple, so there are all sorts of variations. Sometimes they're sliced super thin on a mandolin, other times more thickly with a knife. You can use all different vinegars, different ratios of sugar and salt, herbs and spices, etc. in them. Whatever goes into the pickle jar, it's always fun to see how the sliced red onion brightens up so intensely when the acid hits it. So beautiful. These pickled red onions are great in salads, of course, but they're also wonderful on all sorts of sandwiches and on cheese boards.

1   Carefully pack the sliced onion into a 1-quart canning jar. You'll most likely need to use a sauerkraut pounder or heavy pestle to smash them down so they fit into the jar.

2   Combine the vinegar, sugar, water, and salt in a small pot. Bring to a boil over high heat, stirring initially to dissolve the sugar. Once the brine is boiling, remove it from the heat and slowly pour it over the onions until they are covered, leaving about 1 inch of headspace. Set aside to cool to room temperature.

3   Once the brine is cooled, push the onions down so that they're covered in the brine (use a fermentation weight if you have one; see page 26) and cover the jar. Wait at least a day before serving. Store the onions in the refrigerator for up to 1 month.

Sunflower Yogurt Ranch Dressing

MAKES ABOUT 1 PINT

I know some people who seem to have as much ranch dressing flowing through them as blood. It wasn't around all that much in my world, so I never got hooked. I really love our herby, garlicky Sunflower Yogurt Ranch Dressing, though, because to me it's ranch done right. It's salty and tangy, and all the fresh herbs and citrus in it make me happy. We're always trying to identify nonvegan foods, like ranch dressing, that our customers couldn't get enough of before they became vegan—things they have a deep nostalgia for—and then come up with our own playful plant-based take.

1   In a blender, add the Sunflower Yogurt, Aquafaba Mayo, lemon zest and juice, onion powder, garlic powder, and pepper, and blend on medium-low for 1 to 2 minutes, or until smooth.

2   Transfer the dressing to a medium bowl. Stir in the dill, chives, and salt.

3   Chill the dressing for at least 1 hour before serving. Store it in the refrigerator for up to 2 weeks.

NOTE: If you use store-bought yogurt, your dressing will be significantly thinner because our yogurt is thicker than most commercial ones, so I'd recommend using 1 cup of yogurt plus ¾ cup mayo.

```
***********************
1¹/₄ cups Sunflower
    Yogurt (page 130) or
    store-bought vegan
    yogurt (see note)
¹/₂ cup Aquafaba Mayo
    (page 201) or store-
    bought vegan mayo
Zest and juice of 1
    lemon
1¹/₂ teaspoons onion
    powder
¹/₂ teaspoon garlic
    powder
¹/₂ teaspoon freshly
    ground black pepper
2 tablespoons minced
    fresh dill leaves
2 tablespoons minced
    fresh chives
¹/₈ to ¹/₄ teaspoon
    kosher salt
***********************
```

𝕱ermenter 𝕻otato 𝕾ala𝕯

****
2¹/₂ pounds Yukon
    Gold potatoes or
    another medium-size
    yellow/gold potato,
    scrubbed and chopped
    into 1- to 2-inch
    pieces
6 bay leaves
1¹/₄ cups Pickle Kraut
    (page 47), chopped,
    or 1¹/₄ cups finely
    diced Sour Dills
    (page 39)
1 to 1¹/₄ cups Aquafaba
    Mayo (page 201) or
    store-bought vegan
    mayo
1 cup finely diced
    yellow onion (about
    1 medium onion)
¹/₂ cup chopped fresh
    dill leaves
¹/₂ cup chopped fresh
    flat-leaf parsley
    leaves
¹/₂ cup chopped fresh
    chives
¹/₄ cup Dijon mustard
¹/₂ to 1 teaspoon
    kosher salt, plus
    more for salting the
    water
¹/₄ to ¹/₂ teaspoon
    freshly ground black
    pepper
****

MAKES 4 TO 6 SERVINGS

I like most potato salads. What I don't like, however, is a dry potato salad with firm potatoes. I love the texture of potatoes in Hawaiian-style salads. Those spuds are almost destroyed—nearly mashed-potato-tender, but not quite. We cook ours just shy of that point for this salad.

What sets our potato salad apart is the addition of chopped Pickle Kraut or finely diced Sour Dills. In the summer, we add a lot of pickle and fresh herbs to it, and when the pickles are no longer around, we switch to kraut. Delicious!

1   Put the potatoes and bay leaves in a large pot and fill it three-quarters full with lightly salted water. Bring to a boil over high heat, and boil the potatoes for 10 to 12 minutes, or until very tender. You want the potatoes at the stage where they could easily be mashed but are still intact.

2   Drain the potatoes in a colander, being careful not to break them apart too much. Discard the bay leaves. Transfer the potatoes to a large bowl and let them cool to room temperature, about 1 hour.

3   Once the potatoes are cool, add the Pickle Kraut, Aquafaba Mayo, onion, dill, parsley, chives, mustard, salt, and pepper. Stir well to combine. Cover and refrigerate for at least 1 hour before serving. Store the potato salad in the refrigerator for up to 1 week.

Aquafaba Mayo

MAKES 1 PINT

You can certainly use any store-bought vegan mayo in lieu of our Aquafaba Mayo in our recipes, but if you've never made your own vegan mayo, I highly recommend giving this one a whirl. It's delicious and keeps refrigerated for a couple weeks so you can make all sorts of delicious Fermenter recipes with it, including our Fermenter Potato Salad, of course, as well as our Sunflower Yogurt Ranch Dressing (page 199) and Kale Dressing (page 192). It'll make you eat more SALAD!

1 In the bowl of a food processor, add the gelled aquafaba and process for 2 to 3 minutes, until it begins to foam up. Depending on how large your food processor is, you might need to tilt it slightly in order for the blade to meet the aquafaba.

2 With the machine still running, add the Apple Cider Vinegar, sugar, mustard, and salt, and process for another 30 seconds.

3 With the machine still running, drizzle in the oil very slowly. This should take you 3 to 4 minutes. Adding the oil this slowly allows the mayo to fully emulsify. Chill for at least 1 hour before using. Store in the refrigerator for up to 2 weeks.

MAKING THE AQUAFABA GEL

If you plan to make our Aquafaba Mayo and our Chickpea Miso (page 61) in tandem, then you'll have aquafaba left over from the miso to make the mayo. Simply use 8 cups of water to soak the 1 cup of chickpeas for the Chickpea Miso (or use the chickpeas for something else: salads, hummus—whatever you want) overnight. Don't strain off the soaking water from the chickpeas. Instead, simmer them in their soaking water in a medium pot over medium-low heat for 30 to 40 minutes, until tender. Don't discard the soaking water—a.k.a. aquafaba—when you strain them.

You should have a little more than 2½ cups of aquafaba. In a small pot over medium-low heat, simmer the aquafaba for 30 to 40 minutes, until it has darkened, thickened, and reduced down to roughly ⅓ to ¼ cup. Remove from the heat and set aside to cool to a gel.

****
$^1/_4$ cup gelled aquafaba (see Making the Aquafaba Gel below)
1 tablespoon Apple Cider Vinegar (page 100) or store-bought cider vinegar
2 teaspoons organic pure cane sugar
1 teaspoon Dijon mustard
1 teaspoon kosher salt
2 to $2^1/_4$ cups sunflower oil or other neutral oil

****

Grilled Shio Koji Asparagus

with Lemony Yogurt Sauce

****

$^1/_2$ cup Sunflower
    Yogurt (page 130) or
    store-bought vegan
    yogurt (see note)
Zest and juice of $^1/_4$
    to $^1/_2$ lemon
$^1/_4$ cup chopped fresh
    parsley leaves, dill
    leaves, or chives,
    divided
$^1/_4$ to $^1/_2$ teaspoon
    kosher salt
3 stalks green garlic,
    thinly sliced, or
    2 scallions plus 1
    clove garlic, thinly
    sliced
2 tablespoons plus 1
    teaspoon sunflower
    oil or other neutral
    oil, divided
1 bunch asparagus
    (about 1$^1/_2$ pounds),
    woody ends (bottom 1
    to 2 inches) snapped
    off (see note)
$^1/_4$ cup Shio Koji (page
    70) or store-bought
    shio koji

****

MAKES 4 TO 6 SERVINGS

I love the simplicity of this dish and how loudly it says spring and summer. Added bonus: if it's too blazing hot for grilling and eating something charred, you can make a few minor adjustments and spin this into a chilled salad. Simply prepare the yogurt sauce, sautéed green garlic, and herb mix, and set them aside. Chop the asparagus into 2- to 3-inch pieces, blanch it in lightly salted boiling water for about 1 minute, then shock it in ice water. Toss the cooled asparagus in the Shio Koji, yogurt sauce, and chopped fresh herbs, and then refrigerate. Now you've got yourself a super-cooling dish for a hot summer day!

You can always sub in other spring veggies; simply adjust the grilling or blanching time accordingly. These flavors and techniques are especially great with carrots, sugar snap peas, turnips, and radishes. Grilled radishes are great, but skip the blanching/shocking step if you want them chilled.

> **NOTE:** If you use store-bought yogurt, your sauce will be significantly thinner because our yogurt is thicker than most commercial ones, so I'd recommend using a little less lemon juice to keep the sauce from being too loose.

1   In a medium bowl, combine the Sunflower Yogurt, lemon zest and juice to taste, 2 tablespoons of the chopped herbs, and the salt. Set aside.

2   In a small pan over medium-low heat, cook the green garlic and 1 teaspoon of the oil for 5 to 6 minutes, stirring regularly until it's fairly wilted. Remove the pan from the heat and set aside.

3   In a wide, slightly deep dish large enough to fit the asparagus, toss the asparagus in the remaining 2 tablespoons of oil.

4   Light your charcoal or gas grill. (I prefer charcoal for this recipe.)
    When it's hot, add the asparagus and grill for 3 to 4 minutes, turning
    the spears once or twice. I like to put them directly on the grill
    grates because I want as much char as possible, but I know it's
    difficult to keep the spears from falling through. You can always use
    a grill basket.

5   Brush the asparagus with the Shio Koji a couple times while
    continuing to grill, turning the spears once or twice, for 3 to 4 more
    minutes, until the asparagus is tender and nicely browned in spots.

6   On a large plate or platter, spoon the yogurt sauce into a loose
    mound in the middle. Place the grilled asparagus on top of the yogurt.
    Top the asparagus with the sautéed green garlic and the remaining 2
    tablespoons of minced herbs. Serve family style.

    NOTE: We're always trying to get closer and closer to zero waste in
    our kitchen (see Waste Not, Want Not, page 54). One way we do that
    is by hanging on to our woody asparagus ends, after we've snapped
    them off the spears. We then roast and juice them for tasty sauces.
    If you want to do this, simply toss them in oil, season with salt and
    pepper to taste, and roast them at 425 degrees F for 25 to 30 minutes,
    or until they're slightly charred and tender. Let them cool, and either
    pass them through a juicer with some water, or blend them with some
    water (just enough to get them moving) for several minutes until
    smooth. Then pass the resulting slurry through a fine-mesh strainer.

Sunshine Cookies

MAKES ABOUT 1 DOZEN COOKIES

When we were gearing up to start Fermenter, we really wanted a super hippie, energy-packed, and gluten-free cookie that was also over the top satisfying. I came home with a cookie I tested that tasted like cardboard, and my wife Jenny offered her expertise in fixing it. She was a pastry chef before she became a nurse and had been eating GF for a couple of years. She's a much better baker than me, in general, and her gluten-free baking is amazing. She developed a delicious cookie with all the ingredients I wanted. Along with the Almost Famous Fermenter Burger (page 163) and The Fermenter Bowl (page 187), it's been on the menu since day one and I've never met anyone who doesn't love it.

True to her old actually-listens-to-Grateful-Dead nickname "Sunshine," Jenny is as bright and warm as the real thing. She's been a nurse for nearly 20 years and works at a children's hospital in the mother-baby unit. To say it's a really difficult job is an understatement. I'm not going to get into the details of what Jenny sees at work on the regular, but there are so many problems that can come up during the birth process. The gist is, it can be really real, and really raw, and she's often dealing with intense life-and-death situations. Jenny's profession has definitely changed my perspective on what "hard work" means. I have nothing but complete respect and admiration for people in her field.

As I continued to hear about my wife's days at work and compared it to my days, I found it more and more difficult to complain. It reminded me of an episode of *That Mitchell and Webb Look*, a British sketch-comedy show, where a married couple compare their days: one husband worked as a pediatric cancer doctor and the other husband worked as an ice cream taster at an ice cream factory. Yeah, so it's impossible for me to take myself too seriously anymore when my biggest problem is whether someone liked their sandwich or not.

Our overall focus as a culture is on celebrity, including celebrity chefs. And that's a shame. There's this incredible glorification of food culture, yet there are people like my wife who actually save babies' lives and no one knows any of their names or the really complicated and difficult, emotionally trying work they do day after day.

Thank you to all the people who save other people's lives and keep us healthy! And here's some sunshine in the form of cookies for you, whether you work in health care or not. I hope they brighten your day, even if just a little bit.

```
*********************
2 cups gluten-free
   traditional oats
1¹/₂ cups gluten-free
   all-purpose flour
   (we prefer Bob's Red
   Mill)
1¹/₄ cups packed brown
   sugar
¹/₂ cup organic pure
   cane sugar
2 tablespoons flaxseed
   meal
1¹/₂ teaspoons baking
   powder
1¹/₂ teaspoons kosher
   salt
1 teaspoon ground
   cinnamon
1 teaspoon ground
   turmeric
¹/₂ teaspoon ground
   nutmeg
²/₃ cup hazelnut butter
¹/₂ cup sunflower oil
   or other neutral oil
```

INGREDIENTS CONTINUED →

1   Preheat the oven to 350 degrees F and line a baking sheet with parchment paper.

2   In a large bowl, mix together the oats, flour, brown sugar, cane sugar, flaxseed meal, baking powder, salt, cinnamon, turmeric, and nutmeg.

3   In a medium bowl, mix together the hazelnut butter, oil, and whey.

4   With a wooden spoon, stir the wet mix into the dry mix until fully incorporated. Fold in the pepitas, blueberries, raisins, sunflower seeds, and hazelnuts.

5   With clean hands, form the dough into 12 balls, each roughly 3½ to 4 ounces. The balls will be the size of small lemons. (When the dough is loose, each cookie measures a bit less than 1 cup.)

6   Using both hands, place a dough ball on the prepared baking sheet and carefully flatten it into a roughly 4-inch-wide, ½-inch-thick round cookie. I find that using one hand to flatten and the other to push the crumbling sides in at the same time works best. Repeat with the remaining balls. This is a very dry cookie mix, which easily crumbles, so you need to be patient.

7   Once you've formed all the cookies, use your hands to sweep up the seeds, fruit, and crumble that have fallen off, and carefully push them back into the cookies.

8   Bake for 15 to 20 minutes, or until the cookies are slightly golden on top and a bit browned on the edges. Aim for closer to 15 minutes for a very chewy cookie and closer to 20 for a crispier cookie.

9   Remove the baking sheet from the oven and cool the cookies completely on the sheet before serving. Please, please do not disturb them before they have completely cooled, or they will crumble. Store at room temperature in an airtight container for up to 1 week.

```
¹/₃ cup hazelnut
   whey (page 138),
   sunflower whey, or a
   plant- or nut-based
   milk
¹/₃ cup pepitas
¹/₄ cup dried
   blueberries
¹/₄ cup raisins
¹/₄ cup sunflower seeds
2 tablespoons toasted,
   chopped hazelnuts
   (see step 1 of our
   Hidden Willamette
   Valley Ranch Salad
   page 197, and do the
   same just in a small
   pan)
***********************
```

Acknowledgments

AARON: Thanks to all the folks at Fermenter who have put up with me through the years. Special thanks to Melissa Watt for being a force to be reckoned with at Fermenter for so many years. Watching you grow into a full-fledged maker was inspiring. Oh, and if you want to see Melissa, they are the superstar in the black T-shirt making our Koji Rice in the process shots on page 64.

To my family, thank you for giving me the space as a young screwup to find my way back and toward a decent direction. Your collective lack of concern over my dead-end career path has allowed me to become the mess of a human being I am today. For that, I sincerely thank you.

To Oi!, punk, and reggae music, thank you for teaching me life lessons about love, loyalty, fairness, and working-class pride. Without you I don't think I'd be the same person. Thanks for being the soundtrack of my working life, forever blasting in my workshop.

To all the amazing makers who have given me advice along the way and shared information and techniques, thank you for guiding me. Special thanks to Alex and Kevin at The Cultured Pickle Shop. Although we spent just a short time together, you have been a huge inspiration. You are a powerful force in this world, and I am better for witnessing it.

Baby Greta and One-Eyed Annie, along with good boy Dash, who has already crossed over the rainbow bridge, have all been the bestest dogs a person could ask for. Each hard day is made a little lighter by your sweet snuggles.

To George Barberis, Tony Ong, and Jill Saginario, thanks for applying your massive talents to this book. I am not one to always believe in myself, so to have you all put your talents behind this project is absolutely astounding. I have so much gratitude for you all.

Thank you, Liz, for being so amazingly patient as we crawled through the creation of this book. We picked a really tough time to try to put this project together. You paused meeting after meeting as we dealt with COVID, staff shortages, personal crises, and a whole mess of other shit that happens when you're running a restaurant even in the best of times. You made this book happen. Thanks for being such a force.

To Jenny Adams, my wife, my love, my everything. I would give up all of this for you. But you'd never ask me to, because you've supported me through all of it. I still can't believe I get to come home, stinking of garlic and vinegar and sauerkraut, and you still think I'm cute. Love you with all my heart. Thank you for your understanding and your patience. Fermenter wouldn't exist without you.

OK BYE!

LIZ: Writing cookbooks is an endurance sport, and so I'd like to thank my energy drink sponsor—all the filled-to-the-brim mugs of delicious Portland-roasted coffee that kept me clickety-clacking, slicing and dicing, and inoculating and incubating throughout this entire project. I couldn't have done this without you!

Thanks to everyone at Sasquatch Books for all your expertise and camaraderie yet again. Always. I love you all so much. Special thanks to our editor extraordinaire, Jill Saginario, who never batted an eye at any of our weird jokes or strange requests. Oh, and special thanks to Tony Ong, who is my favorite book designer to work with. So talented.

Thank you, George Barberis, for this book's gorgeous and playful photos, and thank you, Andrea Sloenecker, for your skilled food styling.

I'm grateful for every Fermenter employee/partner past and present who influenced and informed this book. You all are the bee's knees.

Thanks to everyone who gave tasting notes for all the tasty treats here cover to cover. It was so fun to feed you and get your feedback. In this regard, special thanks to the apple of my eye, Jimbo, who does not love all things fermented, and especially does not love having a spoonful or forkful of something particularly funky and fermented pushed toward him first thing in the morning in the kitchen—"Try it!!" (a thick slice of smoky Koji Beets, a spoonful of sour and big-flavored fermented squash guts, a sipper of turmeric-loaded Boneless Broth)—but who does love me. For that I'm so grateful.

Thanks forevermore to my agent, Kimberly Witherspoon, who was excited about this book from the moment I told her about it. I will always pinch myself over getting to be represented by you. Thank you.

Aaron, your recipes, stories, and life lessons have taught me a lot, and I'm grateful that we got to do this book together. I've loved your cooking since my first bite of it—a bite of your eggplant-pistachio ravioli smothered in tomato–red pepper ragout, to be precise—at your first Portland restaurant, Portobello, which I reviewed in 2009 several months after you opened (all the stars, all thumbs-up). Putting this cookbook together during a global pandemic was chaotic, stressful, and not without drama, but hey, we're family now and will be forevermore. I love you.

Finally, thank you to our sparkling, brilliant, adventurous, and diverse fermentation community near and far, especially Sandor Katz, who visited us and did various Portland book events at Fermenter and beyond in late 2021 when we were deep into the book, and when we all needed some communal fun, some fizzy hope. And thanks to the perennial Portland Fermentation Festival community. I love all of you funky ones so much. Your wisdom and passion are, of course, fizzed and fermented into this one.

Resources

BIO'C CO.: Our go-to for koji spores.
Bioc.co.jp/en

BRØD & TAYLOR: Maker of our favorite at-home fermentation incubator, the Folding Proofer & Slow Cooker (page 23).
BrodandTaylor.com

THE CHEESEMAKER: Vegan cheese cultures central.
TheCheesemaker.com

THE CULTURED PICKLE SHOP: The world's best fermented-pickle shop!
CulturedPickleShop.com

CULTURES FOR HEALTH: Offers a wide variety of fermentation cultures (kefir grains, kombucha SCOBYs, etc.) and some tools.
CulturesforHealth.com

GEM CULTURES: A great source in the United States for koji spores, along with all sorts of other culture sets.
GemCultures.com

KOMBUCHA KAMP: For kombucha, kefir, and other fermented-beverage cultures.
KombuchaKamp.com

MODERNIST PANTRY: We love their Druids Grove line of vegan ingredients.
ModernistPantry.com

MOUNTAIN ROSE HERBS: Organic and sustainable high-quality herbs, spices, teas, and more in Eugene, Oregon.
MountainRoseHerbs.com

NATURESPIRIT HERBS: Wonderful wildcrafted seaweed and herb source. We especially love their Six Mix Seaweed Powder for our North Coast Kraut (page 45).
NatureSpiritHerbs.com

PRESERVED: Great shop for fermentation supplies in Oakland, California.
PreservedGoods.com

RAPRIMA: Source of the best tempeh spores in the world! From Indonesia!
Raprima.com

THE SAUSAGE MAKER: Get your vegan collagen sausage casings here. We usually use 23 mm.
SausageMaker.com

STEELPORT KNIFE COMPANY: We love these Portland-made knives for their sharpness and durabililty, not to mention they are the only cold-forged blades made in the United States.
SteelportKnife.com

WILD FERMENTATION: All sorts of information and amazingness from fermentation guru Sandor Katz.
WildFermentation.com

Index

Page numbers in *italic* refer to photographs.

Printed in China

SASQUATCH BOOKS with colophon is a registered trademark of Penguin Random House LLC

27 26 25 24 23   9 8 7 6 5 4 3 2 1

Editor: Jill Saginario
Production editor: Peggy Gannon
Photographer: George Barberis
Designer: Tony Ong
Food stylist: Andrea Slonecker

Photo on pages ii-iii: ©Mariia / Adobe Stock

Library of Congress Cataloging-in-Publication Data

Names: Adams, Aaron, (Chef) author. | Crain, Liz, author.
Title: Fermenter : DIY fermentation for vegan fare / Aaron Adams & Liz
  Crain.
Description: Seattle, WA : Sasquatch Books, [2023]
Identifiers: LCCN 2022047574 (print) | LCCN 2022047575 (ebook) | ISBN
  9781632174710 (trade paperback) | ISBN 9781632174727 (epub)
Subjects: LCSH: Cooking (Fermented foods) | Fermented foods. | LCGFT:
  Cookbooks.
Classification: LCC TX827.5 .A33 2023 (print) | LCC TX827.5 (ebook) | DDC
  664/.024--dc23/eng/20221122
LC record available at https://lccn.loc.gov/2022047574
LC ebook record available at https://lccn.loc.gov/2022047575

The recipes contained in this book have been created for the ingredients and techniques indicated. Neither publisher nor author is responsible for your specific health or allergy needs that may require supervision. Nor are publisher and author responsible for any adverse reactions you may have to the recipes contained in the book, whether you follow them as written or modify them to suit your personal dietary needs or tastes.

ISBN: 978-1-63217-471-0

Sasquatch Books
1325 Fourth Avenue, Suite 1025
Seattle, WA 98101

SasquatchBooks.com

MIX
Paper from responsible sources
FSC® C169965